CAMBRIDGE LIBRARY COLLECTION

Books of enduring scholarly value

History

The books reissued in this series include accounts of historical events and movements by eye-witnesses and contemporaries, as well as landmark studies that assembled significant source materials or developed new historiographical methods. The series includes work in social, political and military history on a wide range of periods and regions, giving modern scholars ready access to influential publications of the past.

An Historical Outline of the Greek Revolution

William Martin Leake (1777–1860) was a British military officer and classical scholar interested in reconstructing the topography of ancient cities. He was a founding member of the Royal Geographical Society and was elected a Fellow of the Royal Society in 1815. After his retirement in 1815 he devoted the rest of his life to topographical and classical studies. First published in 1826, this second edition contains a detailed discussion of the historical background of and events during the first years of the Greek Revolution (1821–30). Focusing on the Peloponnese, Leake explores the political and social condition of Greece under the Ottoman Empire, discussing the causes of the Revolution and providing a detailed narrative of its course. This volume, the first scholarly work on the subject, provides a valuable contemporary account by an author who was familiar with both the territory and the peoples that were his subject.

Cambridge University Press has long been a pioneer in the reissuing of out-of-print titles from its own backlist, producing digital reprints of books that are still sought after by scholars and students but could not be reprinted economically using traditional technology. The Cambridge Library Collection extends this activity to a wider range of books which are still of importance to researchers and professionals, either for the source material they contain, or as landmarks in the history of their academic discipline.

Drawing from the world-renowned collections in the Cambridge University Library, and guided by the advice of experts in each subject area, Cambridge University Press is using state-of-the-art scanning machines in its own Printing House to capture the content of each book selected for inclusion. The files are processed to give a consistently clear, crisp image, and the books finished to the high quality standard for which the Press is recognised around the world. The latest print-on-demand technology ensures that the books will remain available indefinitely, and that orders for single or multiple copies can quickly be supplied.

The Cambridge Library Collection will bring back to life books of enduring scholarly value (including out-of-copyright works originally issued by other publishers) across a wide range of disciplines in the humanities and social sciences and in science and technology.

An Historical Outline of the Greek Revolution

With a Few Remarks on the Present State of Affairs in That Country

William Martin Leake

CAMBRIDGE UNIVERSITY PRESS

Cambridge, New York, Melbourne, Madrid, Cape Town, Singapore,
São Paolo, Delhi, Dubai, Tokyo, Mexico City

Published in the United States of America by Cambridge University Press, New York

www.cambridge.org
Information on this title: www.cambridge.org/9781108021258

© in this compilation Cambridge University Press 2010

This edition first published 1826
This digitally printed version 2010

ISBN 978-1-108-02125-8 Paperback

AN

HISTORICAL OUTLINE

OF THE

GREEK REVOLUTION,

WITH

A FEW REMARKS ON THE PRESENT STATE OF
AFFAIRS IN THAT COUNTRY.

BY

WILLIAM MARTIN LEAKE,

LATE LIEUTENANT-COLONEL IN THE ROYAL ARTILLERY.

LONDON:

JOHN MURRAY, ALBEMARLE STREET.

MDCCCXXVI.

PREFACE

THE following Memoir has been written at three
different periods, as the dates will show. The
first part having been prepared for a periodical
work, and published anonymously with scarcely
any alteration, is often expressed in a tone somewhat different from that which the author would
have been inclined to employ under his own name.
The work is chiefly addressed to the military
reader, who may be asked after perusing it, whether—considering on one side the character of
the insurgents and the strength of their country,
on the other the imbecillity of the enemy and the
difficulties of his military combinations—he thinks
it possible that the Porte can ever suppress the
Greek insurrection without foreign assistance.
But this foreign assistance is not wanting.

While England, scrupulously observant of her professions of neutrality, seizes in her ports supplies purchased for the use of the Greeks, and outlaws every Englishman that may engage in their cause, French officers by hundreds discipline and lead the Turkish armies, and ships under the Austrian and other flags convey them to the Moréa.

LONDON, *January*, 1826.

PREFACE

THE following pages were ready for the press in the month of September last, but circumstances, over which the Author had no controul, have prevented the publication until the present time. The reader will find it necessary to bear this fact in mind, in the perusal of some parts of the work. If it has lost any interest by the delay, an opportunity has, on the other hand, been thus acquired, of adding a statement of the principal events which have occurred in Greece to the close of the fourth campaign of the Insurrection.

In regard to the Map, it may be right to mention, that the scale and general outline have been borrowed from the " *Ancient Greece*" of M. Barbié du Bocage, which, in the year 1811,

accompanied a new edition of the " Jeune Ana-
charsis" of Barthelemy; but many corrections
have been made in the details of that delineation,
and the names have been inserted solely with a
view to illustrate the present publication.

LONDON, *January*, 1825.

Key to following pages.

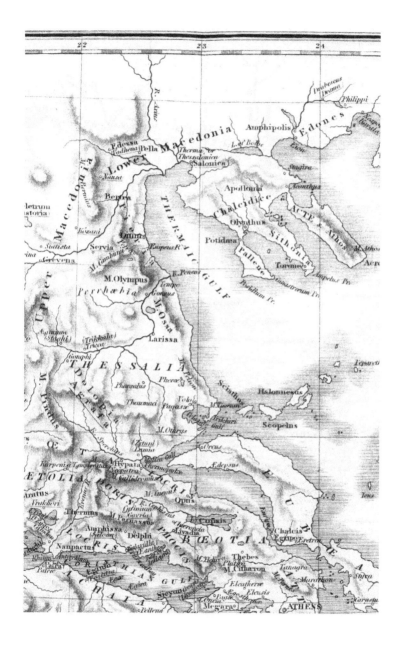

2

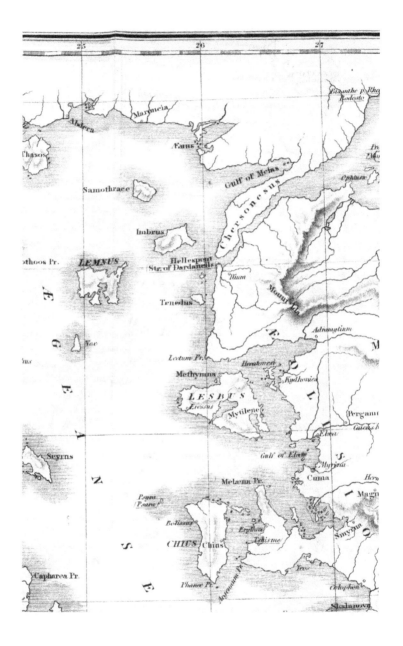

25 26 27

Bisanthe p. Rho
Rodosto

Maroncia

Abdera

Fanis

Chasos

Gulf of Melas

Ophium

Samothrace

C h e r s o n e s u s

Imbrus

othoos Pr.

LEMNUS

Hellespont
Str. of Dardanells

Ilium

Tenedus

Mount Ida

Adramytium

Lae

Lectum Pr.

Heraklonesi

Kydhonies

Methymna

A Æ

Eressus

LESBUS

Mytilene

Pergamu

Caicus R.

Elæa

G

Myrina

Gulf of Elœa

Cuma

Hera

Scyrns

Melena Pr.

Psyra
Psara

Bolissus

Erythræ

Smyrna

Magn

Phismo

CHIUS Chius

S

Capharea Pr.

Planæ Pr.

Tros

Colophon

Argenuusæ Pr.

Sedmowe

3

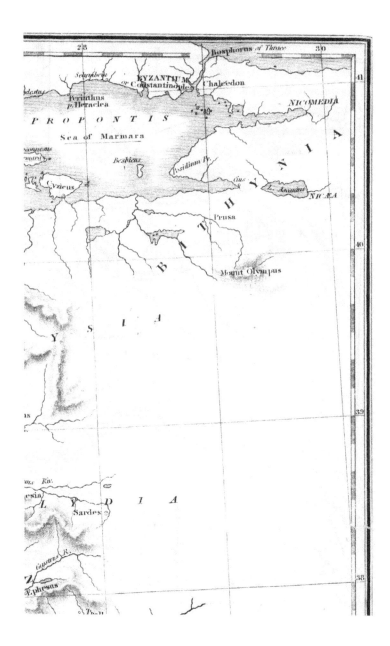

4

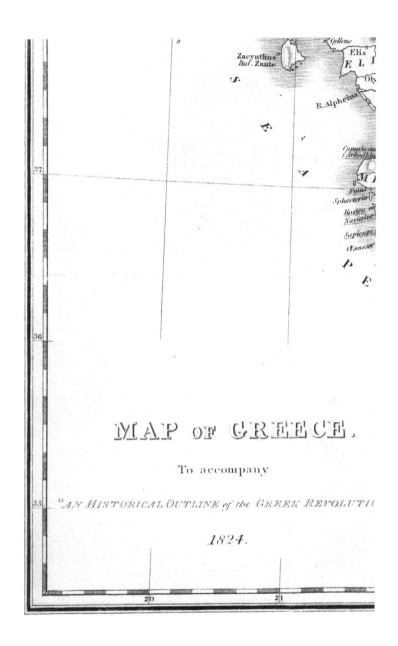

MAP OF GREECE.

To accompany

"AN HISTORICAL OUTLINE of the GREEK REVOLUTIO

1824.

5

Published as the act directs Jan.ʳ 14ᵗʰ 1825 b

v John Murray Albemarle Street London

7

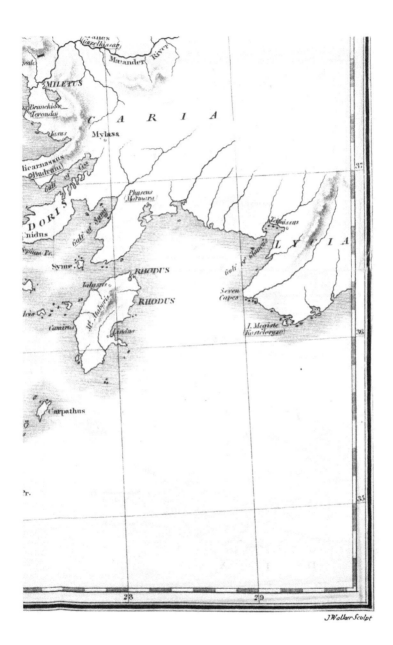

MILETUS

Branchidæ
Terondur

Iasus Mylasa

C A R I A

Maeander River

Gazelhissar

Halicarnassus
Budrum Gulf of Cos

D O R I S

nidus

Phuscus
Marmara

L Y C I A

Telmissus

Symi

RHODUS

Gulf of Macri

Cynian Pr.

Ialysus

Seven
Capes

Camirus Mt. Atabiris

RHODUS

Lindus

I. Megiste
Kastelorgzo

36

Carpathus

r.

35

28

29

J. Walker Sculpt

8

HISTORICAL OUTLINE,

&c. &c.

———————

THERE is no nation, as far as history has left us the means of judging, that has so little changed in a long course of ages as the Greeks. It may be sufficient, without adverting to the less certain indications of manners or physical aspect, to remark, that the Greeks still employ the same character in writing which was used in the remotest age of their history; that their language has received only such corruptions as cannot fail, for the greater part, to fall into disuse, as literary education and a familiarity with their ancient writers shall be diffused among them; that a great number of places in Greece, as well as of the productions of nature, are known by the same names which were attached to them in the most

B

ancient times; and that this language and this
people still occupy the same country, which was
always peculiarly considered among them as
Hellas, or Greece properly so called, namely,
the south-eastern extremity of Europe from the
Tænarian promontory to upper Macedonia, together with the islands and coasts of the Ægæan sea.

Nor are their eastern neighbours much altered,
when we consider the state of Asia in comparison
with that great change which civilization has effected in the human species, and on the surface
of the earth throughout the greater part of Europe. The countries of western Asia are undoubtedly, like Greece itself, less populous, less
opulent, and more barbarous than they were
twenty or thirty centuries ago; but we find that,
notwithstanding the vicissitudes which have occurred among the Asiatic nations themselves, the
Persian of the present day closely resembles, both
in features and dress, his ancestor, as represented
on the walls of Persepolis; and that, although
the predominant power in western Asia has passed
into the hands of a different race of Asiatics, the
strongest general affinity still prevails between
the ancient and the modern inhabitants in cha-

racter, in manners, and in customs, both civil and
military.

The present contest between the Turks and
their late subjects in Greece is probably the
beginning of a new change in that preponderancy
which has been alternating between south-eastern
Europe and western Asia, since the earliest re-
cords of history.

By the successful resistance of the Greeks to
the great Oriental invasion of that country under
Darius and Xerxes, the invaded people raised
themselves to as high a degree of glory, civilization, and intellectual enjoyment as it is possible,
perhaps, for a nation to attain, deprived as they
were of revealed religion, and of all the modern
improvements in science.   By their superiority
in the art of war they were soon enabled not
only to attack their former invaders, but to carry
their victorious arms into the heart of Asia.
From this height, they gradually and inevitably
declined, as the sun declines from the meridian,
until, having first lost their own military spirit
and skill and then the martial discipline which
they learnt in the service of their Roman conquerors, they became unable to contend with the
ferocious valour of the people of Asia inspired by

religious zeal and guided by the energy of the
early Ottoman sultans, and at length fell under
the attacks of the Asiatic barbarians, nineteen
centuries after the former invasion. The situation in which the two people have been placed
for the last 400 years has now produced a new
revolution. While luxuries, chiefly borrowed
from the conquered people, added to the effects
of a general decline of Musulman enthusiasm,
have led to the degeneracy of the Asiatic masters
of Greece, their subjects have been so much improved by adversity, and by the light transmitted
from Christendom, that the Oriental invaders are
once more threatened with expulsion from Europe.

It is but a very few years since the Greeks had
no higher views than the hope of witnessing the
downfall of their oppressors, and of obtaining an
easier yoke under the conqueror, often applying
to themselves the humble language of the vine to
the goat, in the elegant epigram of Evenus:—

Κἤν με φάγῃς ἐπὶ ῥίζαν, ὅμως ἔτι καρποφορήσω
᾿Οσσον ἐπισπεῖσαί, σοι, τράγε, θυομένῳ.

But they now seem to think of sacrificing the
goat themselves.

While their mountaineers and seamen are as-
serting the cause of independence in arms, many
a lettered Greek is undoubtedly engaged in no-
ticing occurrences as they come under his immediate observation.   Until these memoirs, together
with those of a few European eye-witnesses, shall
be collected, we can hardly hope to obtain correct
particulars of a series of events, which are not
less interesting from their scene of action, than
from their singularity, compared with the common
course of modern history: for as to those mixed
compilations of truth and error called Histories
or Memoirs of the Revolution, which have been
published in several of the capitals of Europe, it
is in vain that the reader attempts to extract from
them any clear and connected description of the
contest.   Their obscurity is not a little heightened
by the defectiveness and inaccuracy of the existing
maps of Greece; as well as by the want of that
authentic guidance to the truth which in civilized
Europe is afforded by the official reports of military transactions, but which it is contrary to the
custom of one of the contending parties to pub-
lish, and the other has not yet been in a state of
government to attend to.   And thus the inquirer,
however diligent, is exposed, almost without re-

source, to that torrent of exaggeration or mistatement, which, without any systematic intention of deceiving on the part of those really engaged in the war, is conveyed to this extremity of Europe from Turkey, the Ionian islands, Italy or Austria; and which, after receiving, perhaps, some further colouring in Paris, or in London itself, is poured forth in an unceasing stream from the daily press.

In the following pages, it is intended to give a brief statement of the origin and progress of the insurrection, and of the principal transactions of the war, to the latest period of which we have intelligence. No attempt will be made to enter into such minute details as cannot yet be obtained with accuracy. The author is acquainted with the scene of action, and with the customs of the two contending parties; and, although he has not been in any part of Greece since the contest began, he has had opportunities of collecting the facts from authentic sources.

As the causes of such an event as the present insurrection in Greece cannot thoroughly be understood without a reference to the previous condition of those who are engaged in it, it will be necessary to detain the reader with a few observations on this subject. It is remarkable that travellers who visit Greece generally return from thence with an unfavourable opinion of the people. But it is not difficult to account for this. From a real or supposed want of time, or in consequence of the disgust and impatience usually produced by the privations and inconveniences of a semi-barbarous state of society, travellers are generally contented to follow the beaten route of Athens, the Islands, the Asiatic coast, Troy, and Constantinople; their journey is concluded before they have acquired a sufficient knowledge of the language to form any impartial estimate of the national character; and they come chiefly into contact with those classes upon which the long subjection of the nation to the Turks has had the greatest effect, such as persons in authority under the government or otherwise in Turkish employ, servants, interpreters, the lower order of traders; and generally the inhabitants of those towns and districts in which the Turkish population has a great preponderance of numbers.

It is obviously not in these situations, but in the more unfrequented islands and on the continent of European Greece, where the Turks do not form a tenth part of the population, that the inquiry ought to be made whether any of the

ancient talents and virtues of the Greeks have sur-
vived the four centuries of Musulman oppression,
which supervened upon the debasement caused
by Byzantine despotism, weakness, and supersti-
tion.   In such an inquiry, it would be further necessary to distinguish between the inhabitants of
the plains and those of the mountains; for these
two classes have been placed in very different
circumstances ever since the establishment of the
Ottoman power in Greece.

As the chief strength of an Asiatic army consists in its cavalry, it was to the skill of the Osmanlys in the management of the horse and the
sabre, added to religious enthusiasm; to the confidence inspired by former success and to their
general superiority in courage and enterprize over
the degenerate Greeks, that they owed the conquest of the Eastern empire of Rome.   But the
horse and the sabre are very imperfect instruments for the subjugation of mountainous districts;
and after the first incursions of the Turks the
mountaineers of Greece were not long in deriving
new means of defence from the increasing use of
fire-arms among them.

The consequence has been that the mountains
of Greece have never been completely subdued

by the Ottomans, and that, while the Christian
inhabitants of the plains either retired before
them, or became mere cultivators for the conquerors, who assumed possession of the lands by
a grant from the sultan upon the feudal tenure
of military service, the inhabitants of the mountains have retained possession of the soil, and,
having been joined by many of the Christians of
the plains, are still nearly as numerous as under
the Byzantine empire. Meanwhile, depopulation,
the effect of lawless oppression and of frequent
visitations of the plague, has produced in many
of the most fertile parts of Greece desolation and
consequent unhealthiness of air, which would
have been still more extensive had not a part of
the vacancy been filled up at different times since
the Turkish conquest by Christian migrations
from Albania and Bulgaria, where local wars,
Musulman persecution, or superabundant numbers in a very poor soil had occasionally caused
distress greater even than that which had driven
the Greeks from their native lands.

About two centuries ago, a large colony of
Christian Albanians settled in Bœotia, Attica, and
Argolis, where their descendants still speak the

Albanian tongue: a small tribe of them, which
passed over into the barren island of Hydrea,
founded the community which has since been so
conspicuous for its commercial enterprize and
opulence.

Of the people of Greece Proper who have been
driven from their native land by the effects of
Turkish oppression, many have migrated during
the last half century to Asia Minor, attracted by
the mild government of the Turkish family of Kara
Osmàn Oglu, under whom numerous Greek towns
enlivened the vallies of the Hermus and Caicus,
and had almost restored that country to the fer-
tility which it enjoyed under the Pergamenian
kings.

The nominal conditions upon which the Christian peasant of European Turkey labours for the
Turkish proprietor are not oppressive: they were
adopted by the Ottomans, among many other
established usages of the country, and the practice
is similar to that which is still very common in all
the poorer countries of Europe.   After the de-
duction of about a seventh for the imperial land-
tax, the landlord receives half the remainder, or
a larger share, according to the proportion of the

seed, stock, and instruments of husbandry, which he may have supplied.*

Nor is the capitation-tax, which the Sultan exacts from every rayah, or non-conforming subject, severe in itself, however vexatious it often proves in the collecting; as it very seldom amounts to so much as two pounds sterling per annum for an entire family.

The Turks, however, by obliging the Christian peasants to dispose of the fruits of their labour for the use of Constantinople, or of the local government, at a price fixed by the purchaser,—by occasional levies of contributions in money or kind, by the quartering of soldiers, by Angária,† or the exaction of gratuitous labour for works called public, and by various other modes of oppression, reduce the profits of the Christian labourer to such a pittance, as hardly leaves him an existence.

Such has been the general condition of the

---

* This mode of farming, like so many other customs in Greece, has prevailed from the earliest ages. The μεϱτικάϱης was known by the name of μοϱτίτης in the time of Solon (Jul. Pol. 7. c. 32.) He is the partiarius or medietarius of the Latins, from which last word comes the French métayer, métairie.

† This word, with its present meaning, is found in Menander, (ap. Suid.) Both the custom and the word were imported into Greece from Persia.

peasantry in the plains of Macedonia, Bœotia and
Thessaly, in Eubœa, and in all those parts of the
country in which the Turks were most numerous.
In the Moréa and other parts of Greece to the
southward of Mount Œta, where the level country is more intersected by mountains, and where
conquest was less complete, the Turks were less
anxious to establish themselves as feudatories,
the convents retained a portion of their landed
property, and some parts even of the vallies have
remained in the hands of the Greeks either as
proprietors or as tenants of the Turkish Emperors,
who set apart some of the best districts of this
part of Greece as imperial domains, or for the
support of the imperial harem, or of the imperial
mosques, or of the female relations of the Sultans.
In these situations the Christians continued to
hold a large portion of the lands on easy conditions; and having greater facility than elsewhere in making their complaints heard at court,
they enjoyed some protection from oppressive
governors.   In all the islands of the Ægæan,
except in some portion of the Asiatic islands of
Rhodes, Cos, and Lesbos, the Greeks have always remained in possession of the lands, subject
only to the land-tax and capitation.

In general, the condition of the peasant under

the Greek proprietor was not much better than
under the Turks themselves. It was the inevitable
effect of the Turkish system to prompt the Greek,
who had acquired power either by property or
by office, to exercise it in the oppression of his
inferiors. Like the Turk, the Greek landed proprietor often took advantage of distresses which
he had himself created, to lend the peasant money
at an exorbitant interest, and by paying himself
with the fruits of the labourer's industry at a low
valuation, thus reduced him to a condition little
better than that of a slave. In the Peloponnesus
especially the *Proesti*, or *Magistrates*, who were
placed in authority over districts where there
were no Turkish inhabitants, or those who farmed
the collection of the taxes from the Turks, were
hardly to be distinguished from them in manners
or in their cruel conduct towards the peasantry.
The most powerful were often in league with the
Pasha to plunder the Christians, and sometimes
were so allied with him in interest, as to contribute,
by opportune petitions from the Peninsula, backed
by those arguments of the purse, without which
nothing is effected at Constantinople, to obtain
for him the renewal of the Pashalik for an additional year or two. These persons, being inte-

rested in the continuance of ignorance and Turkish
tyranny, were, together with some of the higher
clergy, the greatest obstacles to national improvement; for the latter class having generally procured their ecclesiastical dignities at a considerable expense, were (except in the greater permanence of their offices) placed in a situation very
similar to that of the Turkish governors of provinces and districts, whose object it necessarily
was to exact from the governed as much as they
possibly could, during their transitory authority.

The want of hands in the plains of Greece
attracted great numbers of labourers during the
harvest, vintage, and olive crop, from the islands
of the Ægæan and Ionian seas, who returned
home at the end of the season with the produce
of their well-paid labour; for the ἡμεροκάματον, or
hire of daily labour, is high in Greece, and on the
occasions just mentioned is of course higher than
usual.

In every part of Greece the peasant's family
derives some resource from the spinning of cotton
and wool, and from the weaving of the coarse
stuffs which serve for the greater part of their
dress and furniture; and though his condition
upon the whole is miserable, he is in general in-

dustrious, much attached to his family, anxious
for the education of his children, and equal, if not
superior, in intelligence to the peasantry of the
most civilized countries of Europe.

That this last distinguished characteristic of
the ancient Greeks is retained by their descendants of every condition has in general been allowed even by those who have received the most
unfavourable impressions of the nation. Among
the most ignorant and uncultivated, and even in
the parts of Greece where the Turkish system
was most oppressive, the observing traveller could
not fail to remark that curiosity, ingenuity, keen-
ness, and elocution, for which the ancient people
was remarkable; and the natural effect of which
upon the present race was an extreme impatience
of their unhappy condition. Not a traveller from
civilized Europe could pass without exciting the
hope that some interference in their favour was in
contemplation, and he never failed to hear from
them many bitter reproaches against us for allowing our fellow-christians to remain enslaved under
the yoke of infidels.

The greater part of the peasantry in the plains
of Northern Greece, and in the neighbourhood
of the great Turkish towns, were unarmed; but

in the more mountainous parts of the country,
and generally in every part of the Moréa, there
was scarcely a house that did not, unless prevented by mere poverty, possess a musket or
pistols, or some kind of weapon of defence. It
was a constant practice among the provincial governors of Greece in all cases of an alarm of war
with any of the Christian powers, to secure
hostages from the principal families, at the same
time that a general decree of the Porte was issued
for disarming the Christian subjects. But in
Greece, to which such an edict was always especially directed, its execution was little more than
nominal: for the Turks, being in general afraid
of venturing into the mountainous parts of the
country, or aware of the ease with which the
Greeks could secrete their arms for the moment,
were always ready to accept of a small pecuniary
compromise; and thus the Sultan's commands
for disarming the Christians, like many other of
his decrees relating to them, ended, at the utmost,
in a contribution to the provincial government.

The most remarkable contrast to the inhabitants of the plains of Greece is to be found in
those islands of the Ægæan sea where there are
no Turkish inhabitants, and in the mountainous

parts of Crete, of Laconia, Arcadia, Ætolia, Locris, Epirus, Thessaly, and Macedonia. Here the Greeks bear the most striking resemblance, both in their virtues and defects, to their illustrious ancestors, as we find them depicted in ancient history—industrious, hardy, enterprizing, heroic, ardently attached to their homes and native country, living upon little or lovers of wine and gaiety as the occasion prompts—sanguine, quick, ingenious, imitative ; but vain, inconstant, envious, treacherous and turbulent. In some of the more mountainous parts of Greece, villages and even whole districts were left to their own management, or rather to that of acknowledged primates, who were responsible for the payment of the ordinary contributions, and who generally farmed those taxes from the Turkish government. In some parts of the mountains, not even the kharadj, or capitation, was regularly paid. In all these places, the principal heads of families had some share in the government, and the executive power was generally in the hands of those who had the greatest riches or most extensive connections. As usually occurs in this form of society, the neighbouring villages, or the leading families in a village, were often engaged in quarrels, which had

c

the important effect of enuring them to the use
of arms.

Such also has been the general condition of the
greater part of Albania, both Musulman and Christian; for although a few great chieftains, confirmed
by the authority of the Porte, have from time to time
established a more despotic authority around some
of the principal towns in Albania, they have never
been sufficiently uncontrolled to avoid the necessity of conforming to the petty interests, disputes,
and alliances incidental to such a state of society.
Even Aly Pasha, who had latterly reduced a large
portion of Albania to obedience, and had acquired
influence in every part of it, was not exempt from
the necessity of often deferring to the national
habits of independent anarchy, and as frequently
obtained his ends by artifice as by the open dis-
play of power.

In the highlands of Greece and Albania, a great
part of the male population is engaged in the care
of sheep and cattle, changing their pasture-ground
according to the season of the year.   Others are
owners and conductors of the numerous horses
and mules, which, in a country where there are no
carriage-roads, are necessary for the transport of
commodities of every kind ; and a large portion of

them are labourers, artisans or shopkeepers in Constantinople and other great towns in Turkey, which are supplied with many of their most industrious inhabitants from the mountains of Greece. The manufactures of Greece are chiefly confined to the most common articles of dress and furniture. Of the very few which are exported, the most remarkable are the capa's, or thick cloaks, of Mounts Pelion and Pindus; the mixed stuffs of silk and cotton, chiefly Thessalian; the red and yellow leather made in several of the great towns both of Northern Greece and the Morèa; and the dyed cotton thread of Mounts Olympus and Ossa, which formed a capital branch of commerce with Germany, Poland, and Russia.

Villages of artisans and traders, who pursue their traffic abroad, are most numerous in the Christian districts of Albania, in Epirus, in the mountains which surround Thessaly, in Ætolia, Arcadia, and Laconia. Some of the largest and most opulent in Northern Greece are remains of the Wallachian colonies, which settled in Greece about the tenth century.

It was generally the practice of all the mountaineers of Greece and Albania, to return to their families as often as their interests would admit,

and ultimately to reside in their native mountains,
where they enjoyed as great a degree of security,
as any part of the Turkish dominions afforded,
until Aly Pasha found means to introduce his
Albanian soldiers among them: for Aly, though
anxious to transmit his acquired authority to his
family, never thought of obtaining this object by
protecting the property of his subjects, or by rendering them interested in the permanence of his
power, and could never divest himself of that avidity for immediate gain, which is the sole guide of
every Turk in office.   While continually augment-
ing his personal landed property at the expense of
both Turks and Greeks in Epirus, Acarnania,
and Western Thessaly, he was equally eager to
plunder of their savings the industrious artisans
and traders of every part of Northern Greece ;
and as this conduct forced them to emigrate, whenever they could escape his vigilance, (for he always
endeavoured to prevent them by force,) the extension of his power had the effect of dispeopling
many towns in Northern Greece, and of depriving
that country of many of its best inhabitants. It is
probable that in the latter years of Aly's reign, the
population of continental Greece, from Cape Tæ-
narum to the northern-most limits, at which the

Greek language is in common use, was not much
greater than a million.

The change which has taken place in the political condition of the Greeks since the Turkish
conquest, has principally arisen from two causes,
both of which have been progressive, ever since
that event. The one is the increase of knowledge,
communicated to the Christians from civilized Europe, while the Turks have been in a stationary
or declining state; the other is the apostacy of
Albania, or the conversion of a great part of its
population from Christianity to the Islam. While
the former effected such a gradual improvement
of a moral and mental kind, as had a direct tendency to rouse the natives of Greece to throw off
the yoke, the latter, being more rapid in its progress, has operated with still more efficacy to prevent such a result.

Next to the preservation of their religion, the
modern Greeks have been indebted for returning
civilization to their foreign commerce. That which
they possessed at the time of the Turkish conquest was not entirely lost after that event, because
the conquerors, unskilful in any thing but arms,
and despising trade, left the pursuit of it to their
Christian subjects. While that of Asia chiefly

fell into the hands of the Armenians, the Greeks, from their position, naturally retained the greater part of the commerce of European Turkey; and hence they came into immediate contact with the increasing improvement of Christian Europe. Numerous families, escaping from Turkish oppression, emigrated into the adjacent countries, and by degrees Greek commercial houses were established in the maritime towns of Europe, or in the interior of Russia and Germany, and they have even spread as far as India.

The communication being constant between the emigrant Greeks of Europe, and those who remained under the Turkish yoke, great efforts were made by the former to meliorate the mental condition of their brethren in Greece: they were warmly seconded by the more enlightened or opulent Greeks of Turkey: many Greeks were educated in Europe, and education gradually spread over Greece, by the establishment or enlargement of schools and colleges.

Even of late years, during which the trade and industry of Northern Greece suffered so much injury from the oppressive government of Aly Pasha, the increase of education among the Greeks has not been proportionably checked, as

Aly found some immediate advantage in favouring education among his Christian subjects; while the Greeks who were driven to settle in the neighbouring parts of civilized Europe, still continued to promote the improvement of their fellow-countrymen, who remained under the yoke.

Notwithstanding the superiority which the Frank merchant enjoyed over the Greek, in paying a single ad valorem duty, of three per cent. on imports and exports, while the rayah, besides being subject to illegal extortions, paid five per cent. in addition to repeated charges on moving his merchandize, the advantage which a native merchant always possesses in economy and local information, had gradually enabled the Greeks to drive the Frank merchants from the fairs of Greece, to obtain a great part of the internal maritime commerce of Turkey, and at length to share very largely in the exchange of the corn, oil, cotton, silk, and other produce of Greece for the manufactured goods and colonial produce of the European nations.

In the latter part of the last century, the foreign commerce of the Greeks had so much increased, that their competition was the principal cause of the decline of the European factories which had

long flourished in the principal Turkish marts:
that competition having been greatly favoured,
against the interests of the Frank merchants, by
their own diplomatic agents, who largely exercised
the privilege of granting protections to the Christian subjects of Turkey, in virtue of which they
enjoyed the same commercial privileges as the
merchants of the protecting state.

The French revolution had a further effect in
promoting the commerce of the Greeks, and with
it the extension of education and knowledge
throughout the nation, by placing in their hands
the greater part of the carrying trade of the Black
Sea and Mediterranean, which had formerly been
enjoyed by the South of France and the Adriatic.

For several years before the present insurrection broke out, there were between four and five
hundred Greek ships employed in the commerce
of the Black Sea; at the same time that colleges
with professorships in various branches of instruction were established at *Kydoniés*, Smyrna, Chios,
Ioannina, besides the smaller establishments at
Patmos, Thessalonica, *Ambelákia*, *Zagorá* (in
Pelion), Athens, *Dimitzána* (in Arcadia), some of
which, although of old date, had been renewed
or increased of late years. It is not surprising,

under these circumstances, that the mental improvement of the Greeks, and the superiority
which it gave them over their unimproveable
masters, had rendered the latter more and more
dependent upon them in the transaction of busi-
ness of every kind.

And here the reflection may be made, that if
Greece should achieve her liberation, she will be
indebted for the return of civilization and independence to the same peculiarities of geographical
position and structure, to the same indelible features of nature, which raised her to greatness in
ancient times. While her extensive sea coast
and numerous islands and harbours rendered her
the country of maritime commerce, and were the
original cause of the opulence which led to per-
fection in the enjoyments and arts of civilized life,
the mountainous structure of the interior gene-
rated that free and martial spirit, which, however
cruelly suppressed, has never been completely
destroyed.

We shall now offer a few remarks on that which
we have already indicated as having had a powerful effect in retarding any movements of the
Greeks for the assertion of their independence—

we mean the increase of the religion of Mohammed in Albania.

Although it cannot be doubted that many
Greeks have abandoned the cross for the crescent,
since the Turkish conquest, and that there is a
considerable proportion of Greek blood in the
present race of Ottomans, as well from the male
as from the female side, it is nevertheless certain
that the Greeks have in general shewn an attachment to their church, very remarkable in their
oppressed state, and highly honourable to the
nation. In return, their church has been a great
consolation to them in their servitude, has maintained union and nationality among them, and, by
preserving the use of the Hellenic in the church
service, has saved their language from the utter
corruption to which it would otherwise have been
exposed from the absence of all Greek literary
education, and from the mixture of the Turkish,
Albanian, and Bulgarian tongues.

The Albanians on the other hand, who are the
remains of the ancient Illyrians, a race in all times
very inferior to the Greeks in the scale of humanity and civilization, and among whom Christianity had probably never taken a very deep root,

have shewn a much slighter regard for their religion since the period of the Ottoman invasion,
although they have not had that degreee of excuse
for their apostacy, which the complete subjugation
of some parts of Greece may be thought to have
afforded to the Greeks. Half the Albanian nation has relinquished the Christian faith for that
of Mohammed. The poverty of the soil prompt-
ing a large portion of the people to seek a subsistence abroad, and the military habits acquired
in their domestic wars leading the greater part of
them to prefer the profession of arms, their reputation as soldiers has increased as the Osmanlys
have degenerated, until they have become the
only effective infantry in the Turkish dominions,
and are to be found in the service of almost every
Turkish chieftain in Europe, Asia, and Africa.

This enterprizing, poor, and mercenary people
was not slow in perceiving the advantages attached to a conformity with the governing religion;
that it opened to them a road to all the distinc-
tions which the Ottoman government affords, or
at least that it facilitated the acquisition of a fortune, with which they might retire to their native
mountains. Some of the chieftains, supported by
their followers, obtained possession of small dis-

tricts in Northern Greece, and even in the Moréa;
while others endeavoured to increase their power
and possessions in Albania, where these acquisitions being generally made at the expense of their
Christian neighbours, numerous families of the
latter were forced to emigrate into Greece and
other parts of Turkey in pursuit of subsistence
by trade or agriculture; while others, sometimes
by whole districts at a time, converted their
churches into mosques, made peace with their
Moslem neighbours, retained their possessions,
and became partakers of the advantages enjoyed
by the profession of the Islam.

The apostacy of Albania having advanced in
an increasing ratio, its effects have been most felt
in the last half century, or at the same time that
the moral and political changes, which we have
already described in the Greeks, have been most
remarkable. When it is considered therefore
that, in this period, insurrections encouraged by
an enemy of the Porte, have twice been quelled
chiefly by the Musulman Albanians, and that the
military strength of the Turkish government in
Greece has of late years been derived almost entirely from them, it seems evident, that it is to the
conversion of so large a proportion of the Alba-

nian nation to the faith of Mohammed, that the
Porte is indebted for having so long been able to
maintain any degree of authority over Greece.

However the Turks may despise the Albanians
as Moslems; however they may detest them for
their superiority in military qualities, and for the
success with which their chieftains have generally
maintained, in defiance of the Porte, their acquired
authority in Greece and Albania, the community
of religious interests which unites all classes of
Mohammedans against Christianity has a corresponding political effect here as well as in every
part of the Musulman world; for it cannot be
doubted that the union of the Ottoman empire
has been not less supported by the common fear
and common hatred of Christians, entertained by
the followers of Mohammed, all of whom, to the
westward of Persia, look to the Sultan as the head
of the church, than by the mutual jealousies of
the great powers of Europe.

It will readily be supposed, from what has been
stated, that the far greater part of the Albanian
soldiers in the service of the Porte, or of the provincial governors in European Turkey, Asia Minor,
Egypt, and Barbary, are Mohammedans.

Some Christian tribes, especially the Roman

Catholics of the north of Albania, are occasionally
found in that situation: but in general, the Christian Albanian soldiers have either remained at
home for the defence of their native districts, or
have entered into the service of the Greek governors of the Ultra-Danubian provinces, or have
joined the bands of robbers which infest various
parts of European Turkey, or have been united
to the Armatolí and Kleftes of Greece.

The Armatolí (ἀρματωλοί), or Greek militia,
was an establishment of the Byzantine empire;
their most important employment was to keep the
roads free from danger, and to guard the Κλει-
σοῦραι, or mountain-passes, which are so frequent
in Greece, and of so much military importance.
The Ottomans found it necessary to maintain the
same kind of police; in some instances the inhabitants of the district adjacent to the passes were
made responsible for the safety of the roads, were
authorized to maintain Armatolí for this purpose;
and, in consideration of the trust and expense,
were allowed certain privileges, such as that of
being exempted from the customary burthen of
entertaining persons travelling in the service, or
under the protection of the government. The
villages of the Elutheris and Megaris, occupying

the approaches to the Isthmus, were thus consti-
tuted, and were hence called the Derveno-Khoria,
from the Persian word Derbend (pass). In addition to the bodies of Armatolí, acknowledged by
the Porte, all the mountain communities, in their
various degrees of submission to the Turkish government, maintained a small body of Armatolí,
for the maintenance of the police, or for the protection of the district, and who were often employed against a neighbouring rival, or still oftener
to resist, or at least to check, the encroachments
of Mohammedan extortion, whether Turkish or
Albanian. And thus there was constantly a
school, however rude, for the military profession
in Greece.

In Northern Greece the Porte had found it
convenient to place the care of all the passes in
the hands of one Dervenjí, or Κλεισουράρχης, as
this officer was called under the Byzantine empire.
It was from his appointment of Dervenjí Bashi,
that Aly Pasha of Ioannina dated his fortune and
his power. Having succeeded in recommending
himself to the Porte, as a fit person to be employed to protect the roads, and to suppress the
the resistance to Turkish authority, which so often
manifested itself among the mountaineers, he

soon, by means of the authority thus acquired,
increased his wealth and his influence in Albania
to such a degree, that the Porte was never able
to take the guardianship of the passes out of his
hands; and he took good care that some com-
plaint of robbers, together with some petition to
the Porte in favour of his holding the office, should
never be wanting, when, in consequence of any
political change at Constantinople, he had reason
to fear the decline of his influence.

He affected to treat all those, who resisted his
authority, as robbers [κλέφταις]; he omitted no
opportunity of boasting of the safety of the roads
within his territories, and in this he generally received the favourable suffrage of the stranger,
who, feeling the benefit of the security derived
from Aly's strong government, might contrast it
with the dangers to which he was often liable in
the Moréa from rebellious Armatolí, who easily
found a retreat from the Turkish power in the
mountains of Laconia and Arcadia.

As the power of Aly extended over Greece,
the greater part of the Armatolí became troops in
his service, contributing to maintain his authority,
and giving him the reputation of preserving security of person and property; but, in fact, allowing

of no plunder but that which was directed by himself for his own sole benefit, and which pervaded every place and in every form of extortion, where his influence was completely established.

As some of the most secluded districts of Northern Greece held out against him to the last, and as his Armatolí were often provoked by his avarice and treachery to join the armed insurgents, his habitual opponents, the Kleftes, were never entirely suppressed. And hence it will easily be understood that the Armatolí and Kleftes of Greece differed only in the circumstances in which they were placed: and that, although the latter were often obliged by necessity to resort to plunder, and to imitate the cruelty of their opponents, they were less to be considered as robbers, than as rebels against the government. Like the pirates of the Ægæan in the early ages of Greece,* their name carried no disgrace with it. On the contrary, their cause being connected with the assertion of national and Christian freedom against infidel oppression, and their life being passed in continual dangers, amidst the most romantic scenery, were calculated to call forth the

* Thucyd. l. i.

poetical and enthusiastic spirit inherent in the
people, and to keep alive among them the love of
liberty and the hope of independence.

As long as a Christian tribe maintained itself
in one of the strongest positions of Northern
Greece, the mountain population maintained in
many places that degree of liberty and self-pro-
tection which it had enjoyed from the time of the
Turkish conquest; but when *Suli*, after a valiant
resistance of thirteen years against all the resources of the power, wealth, craft, and treachery
of Aly, had sunk under the effects of famine and
deficient numbers, his influence found its way into
every part of Northern Greece, and left very few
retreats in which the Greeks could enjoy the
fruits of their industry in safety.

It was most fortunate for the Ottoman government, that when the causes, which have at length
produced a general insurrection, had begun to
operate very extensively, and when the French
revolution, and the ambition of its leaders, threatened the Porte with an immediate explosion, the
military strength of Greece and Albania was more
concentrated than ever.

Aly Pasha may have thwarted the execution
of all the measures of the Porte which tended to

reduce his authority, and in general those which did not originate with himself; he may have transmitted a larger sum to Constantinople in the shape of presents to persons in power, than in that of tribute to the imperial treasury; and, in the latter respect, he may never have sent as much as satisfied the wishes of government; nevertheless it is probable that the Porte, during his reign, was more truly master of Greece than it had ever been before, and that it derived, upon the whole, as much revenue from the country; while it is certain, that by leaving Aly to oppose the armed Greeks to one another, and to suppress the spirit of revolt by the military strength of Albania, she most effectually secured herself against the consequences of foreign intrigues among the Christian subjects of European Turkey; and that the concentration of power in Aly's hands was the best protection which the empire could possess on a frontier, where it was endangered by the increase of the power of France, not less than the North-Eeastern side was menaced by the encroachments of Russia.

We may now proceed to lay before the reader a brief narrative of the origin and progress of the Greek insurrection.

No sooner had the present Sultan Mahmoud
been placed upon the throne, than he began to
indicate talents and a temper not easily directed
by others, together with an intention of pursuing
a line of policy, which, founded on Mohammedan
bigotry, and on ignorance of the real situation of
his empire, was less suited to his own times than
to those of Selim the First or Solyman the Second.
One of his favourite projects was the destruction
of the great chieftains who, in several of the provinces, partly from motives of ambition, and partly
in their own defence against the avidity and treachery of the Porte, had retained their offices for
a long succession of years, in opposition to all the
attempts of the supreme government to remove
them, gradually increasing the circle of their
power, placing their relations and dependents in
subordinate situations around them, and in some
instances transmitting their authority to their
heirs.

This usurpation of power by a few strong
hands, although at once both a consequence and
a cause of the weakness of the Ottoman government, had, as we have already hinted, been the
best security of the empire, during the dangers
of the French revolution; and, if prudently ma-

naged, might still have saved it for some time
from the effects of the degeneracy of the people,
both as Moslems and as soldiers, which, when
contrasted with the great advances made by
Christian Europe in military power and the art
of war, has now for many years threatened Turkey with the most imminent danger. But the
Porte, blind to more important considerations,
was sensible only to wounded pride and to the
loss of immediate authority and revenue. Before
Mahmoud had been ten years on the throne,
none of the great permanent provincial governors
remained, except Aly of Ioannina and Mohammed
Aly of Egypt, the latter of whom can hardly
enter into consideration on this occasion, Egypt
having seldom been thoroughly under the domi-
nion of the Porte, but generally in an intermediate state between the submission of the Ottoman provinces and the mere nominal subjection
of the Barbary states.

It was not until after the general pacification of
Europe, that the Sultan and his favourite coun-
sellors, finding the Albanian Aly no longer important in the protection of the North-Western
frontier of the empire, and impatient to obtain his
treasures before his death should place them in

the hands of his sons, began their operations against him by favouring his enemy Ismaïl Pashó Bey, who, no longer daring to reside at Ioannina, had become a fugitive at Constantinople. An imprudent attempt of some emissaries of Aly in the spring of 1820 to assassinate Ismaïl, became the chief ostensible cause of the Firmahn which was immediately issued against Aly, and which was followed by the appointment of Ismaïl to the Pashalik of Ioannina, and to the command of the army which was destined to reduce that place.

As in every great revolution, it is found that many concurrent causes prepare the way, but that one fortuitous event determines the period of its commencement, so it cannot be doubted that the declaration of the Porte against Aly was the immediate cause of the Greek insurrection. The great preparing cause, as we have already seen, was the degeneracy of the one people and the improvement of the other: the recent example of Spanish America, of Spain itself, of Portugal, and of Italy, formed undoubtedly another link in the chain of circumstances, destined by Providence to bring about this event.

The Greeks residing in Europe had naturally been in the habit of looking chiefly to Russia as

the means by which their country was to be liberated, and at the beginning of the year 1820, the
increasing disagreement between the court of St.
Petersburgh and the Porte had revived the hopes
which rested on this foundation. Already had
some of the adherents of Russia in Greece endeavoured to anticipate the views of that cabinet by
preparing the people for a connection with Russia
in case of a war, and the proceeding easily obtained credit for being authorized, whether it
really were so or not, when a Greek was the
foreign minister of the Emperor Alexander.

Such was the state of affairs when the rupture
between Aly Pasha and the Porte at once made
it evident to those best acquainted with the country that it would be impossible for the Porte ever
to bring back Greece to its former state of subor-
dination. If it required the powerful arm of Aly
to maintain order in Northern Greece, and an
annual visit of the Turkish fleet to the Moréa, to
suppress the spirit of revolt in that peninsula, and
to keep the mountaineers of Laconia in a state of
half submission, what was to be expected when it
became the interest of Aly to attract the armed
Greeks and Albanians to his side against the
Porte, and when the Turkish navy should be

crippled by the desertion of the Greeks, who formed the most numerous as well as most skilful portion of its seamen?

The first step of Aly, on receiving the firmahn of the Porte, which declared him a rebel, was to concert operations with the Greek chiefs who had been under his command as Dervenjí, and who occupied, with their Armatolí, all the mountainous parts of Greece beyond the Isthmus, and especially the passes which lead from every quarter into the basin of Thessaly. The Turks, on their side, were equally sensible of the importance of these mountainous districts in the contest which the Porte had undertaken. Suleyman Pasha, on entering Thessaly as Seraskier, resorted to the dangerous expedient of addressing a proclamation to the ecclesiastics, the civil primates, and other persons in authority in Thessaly and the adjoining mountains, authorizing the people to take up arms against Aly. It has been supposed, however, that this measure was either an unauthorized act of the Turkish commander, of which the Porte disapproved, or that it was an intrigue not thoroughly known to Suleyman himself, but devised by his Greek secretary, who issued the ploclamation in his *own* language only; for the

Seraskier was very soon removed from his command, and beheaded.

But the consequences were not to be remedied : the Greeks, authorized to take up arms, and appealed to on both sides, were not slow either in perceiving the advantages that might be derived from these circumstances to the nation, or in preparing to make them available. Nor was it long before they had sufficient provocation to turn their arms against the Osmanlys: for no sooner had these lawless troops entered Greece than they ravaged all the plains of Thessaly, Phocis, Bœotia, and Attica, and drove great numbers of defenceless inhabitants to seek refuge in the mountains.

Aly experienced the usual fate of selfish tyrants when fortune turns against them. In less than six months after the Porte had issued the proscription against him, he had been abandoned by his allies, his chief officers had betrayed him, and of his mercenary troops, the Christians had retired into their native districts, while the greater part of the Musulmans had entered the service of the Turkish Pasha before *Ioannina.* Scarcely had a division of the Ottoman fleet made its appearance on the western coast of Greece, when two of Aly's sons and one of his grandsons surrendered themselves and the fortresses of *Prévyza*, and *Parga*,* into the hands of the Turkish Admiral, who soon persuaded also the elder son, Muktar, to follow the example of his brothers, and to give up the strong fortress of Argyró Kastro, into which he had retired after having abandoned the still more important post of Beráti, and to accept in exchange a nominal government in Asia Minor, destined of course to be his grave if he should ever be permitted to reach it.

Aly now gave the strongest proof that his hopes rested solely on the armed Christians, by surrendering to the Suliotes the castle which he had built on the site of one of those strong holds from whence it had been the occupation of a great part of his life to expel them ; and the winter of 1820-1 had hardly expired before he perceived, that he had become little more than an instrument in the hands of the Greeks for the recovery of their independence. Such was the position of affairs when an occurrence in the ultra-Danubian provinces of Turkey had a powerful effect in promoting the insurrection of Greece. An association

* Naupactus had been evacuated by Aly's second son, Vely Pasha, and had been occupied by an officer of the Porte, before the Turkish fleet arrived on the coast.

of Greeks, styling itself the Society of Friends,
(ἡ ἑταιρεῖα φιλικὴ) had been formed in the dominions of Austria and Russia about the year 1814,
in imitation of the revolutionary societies then
prevalent in Italy and Germany. The liberation
and revival of Greece, which, in fact, had always
been the ultimate object of the exertions made by
the Greeks residing in civilized Europe, in favour
of their brethren in Turkey, was the design to
which the members of the Hetæreia bound themselves by oath to devote their lives and fortunes.
Inflamed by the revolutionary state of Europe in
the year 1820, the association thought that the
quarrel between Aly and the Porte, the seditious
attitude of Servia, and the discontents of Wallachia and Moldavia, which, in February, 1821, had
broken out into open acts of violence, presented
the desired crisis for attempting a general insurrection of the Christian population of Turkey
against their Mohammedan oppressors. On the
7th of March, 1821, Alexander Ypsilanti, a Major
General in the Russian service, and son of a former Greek governor of Wallachia, entered Moldavia with a corps of Greeks, and in concert with
Michael Sutzo, the reigning Greek governor of
that province, issued a proclamation inviting the

Christians to arms, and promising them in not very ambiguous terms the support of Russia.

But the spirit of discontent in the two Dacian provinces having been chiefly directed against the oppression of the Boyars or native aristocracy, and against the Greek government itself in the exercise of its delegated power, was productive of little or no assistance to Ypsilanti's proceedings. The Servians were equally inefficient, and the Emperor Alexander, who was then at Laybach, having immediately disavowed the proceedings of Ypsilanti and Sutzo, the issue of the attempt could not long be doubtful; after some acts of cruelty perpetrated on both sides, the expedition ended in the evacuation of Yassy by Ypsilanti, and of Bukarest by Theodore, chief of the Vlakho-Moldavian insurgents, whom Ypsilanti shortly afterwards seized, and put to death, he himself retreating after an action in which the Greeks are stated to have conducted themselves gallantly, into the Austrian dominions, where he was immediately seized by the government and immured in a dungeon.

Transitory as were the effects of this rash and ill-conducted enterprise in the Dacian provinces, it had the greatest influence in exciting the insur-

rection in Greece, properly so called, where the
war in Epirus, and the hopes, the movements, and
the designs which had been its consequence
throughout Northern Greece, had already produced a corresponding ferment in the *Moréa.*
The first open act of rebellion in the peninsula
was caused by some tardy steps taken by the provincial government at *Tripolitza* to execute the
decree of the Porte, customary in all cases of
alarm, for disarming the Christians and for receiving hostages from the principal families and
churchmen. The example of resistance was set in
the end of March by Germanós, bishop of Patræ,
who having been summoned to the capital, had
proceeded as far as *Kalávryta,** when finding the
people, together with a body of Armatolí, well
disposed to his views, he openly raised the standard of independence and of the Cross, which was
immediately followed by a similar manifestation at
Patræ.†   The *Maniátes,* descending from Mount

---

* The ancient Cynætheia, an Arcadian city on the frontier
of Achaia. We have preferred using the ancient names,
wherever it can be done without ambiguity, because they are
more defined and better known. The italic print has been
employed to distinguish the modern names, whenever the dis-
tinction has appeared necessary.

† This attempt had no other effect than to cause the de-

Taygetum, speedily occupied the level districts of
Laconia and Messenia. Before the end of April
a senate had assembled at *Kalamáta*, in Messenia,
on the borders of *Máni*, and the fleet of *Ydra*,
raising the standard of the Cross, proceeded to
Psará, which, strong in its fortified rock and numerous ships, had been among the first to set the
example of insurrection, although situated on the
advanced posts of the enemy.*

After such simultaneous movements of rebellion
at the two extremities of European Turkey, it
was impossible to persuade the Turks that Russia
had not an extensive design against them by the
agency of their Christian population, and it would
hardly have been in the power of the Porte to
prevent its Musulman subjects from. persecuting
the numerous defenceless Christians who inhabit

struction of the town ; for the garrison of the castle, having
been speedily reinforced by Yussuf Pasha from Naupactus,
and by the Albanian colony of *Lalla*, which was obliged to
retreat before the insurgents, has been able to hold out ever
since.

* Psara (τὰ Ψαρά), called ἡ Ψυρία in the Odyssey, was already
approaching its modern form of denomination in the time of
Strabo, who writes it τὰ Ψύρα. Its harbour, and its position
five miles from the north-west cape of Chios, in the main
channel of the Ægæan, has in all times given some importance to this little island.

the capital, the towns and villages of Thrace, and the Western part of Asia Minor, even had the government been so disposed. But Sultan Mahmoud and his favourites, as if determined to provoke a general insurrection, themselves set the example of persecution, and by stamping it with the mark of religious hatred, were sure to find a ready instrument of their cruel vengeance in every Moslem of the empire. On the 22d April, being Easter-day, the greatest of the Greek festivals, Gregorios, Patriarch of Constantinople, the head of the Greek church, acknowledged and appointed by the Porte, and who had recently issued his anathema against the insurgents, was seized and hanged before the patriarchal church in which he had been officiating ; and as a consummation of ignominy in the eyes of the Greeks, his body was delivered to Jews to be dragged through the streets. And this murder was accompanied, or speedily followed, by that of several other ecclesiastics of the highest rank in the capital, or other parts of the empire, as well as by that of many other Greeks of every class.

The indignation and terror produced among the Greeks by these cruelties, were greatly heightened by the accompanying destruction of several

Greek churches, and a general conviction prevailed
that they were but a prelude to an intended ex-
termination of the whole people. The priesthood
of the islands and of the Moréa, thinking themselves peculiarly marked out for destruction, hesi-
tated not to increase the ferment by their spiritual
influence; and while they represented the patriarch as a *martyr*, and inspired the rebellion with
all the energy of religious warfare, the insurgents
derived no small additional encouragement from
the intimate persuasion that Russia was on the eve
of a rupture with the Porte.

Ydra, Psarú, and *Petza**, were able to enter
upon the naval campaign with a force of eighty or
ninety vessels, of the average bulk of 250 tons,
and the average strength of 12 guns. Fifty or
sixty others of a somewhat smaller class, and
many others still smaller, were supplied by the
other islands, among the foremost of which may
be reckoned Andrus, Scopelus, Myconus, Patmus,
Casus, and Megiste now *Kastelóryzo,* on the
coast of Lycia. In the latter end of May, the
inferiority of the Turkish commanders and seamen
in skill and enterprise was shown in the loss of one
of their two-decked ships of war, which, having

---

* Better known by the Italian appellation of *Spetzia.*

been separated from the Turkish squadron near
Lesbus, was stranded in endeavouring to escape
from the Greeks at Eressus, on the western side
of that island, and was there burnt by a fire-ship
of *Ydra*.

If the events of 1820 had proved that the power
of Aly Pasha rested on a basis of sand, those of
1821 shewed that the authority of the Porte in
Greece was equally unstable. Soon after midsummer, not only in the Peloponnesus, but throughout a great part of Northern Greece, as far as
Thessalonica, the Turks had retired into the large
towns and fortified places, and all the mountains
and open country were either in the hands of the
Greeks or exposed to their incursions. Agents
had been sent to Europe for the purchase of arms
and ammunition ; many volunteers, as well Greeks
as natives of civilized Europe, had arrived in the
Moréa; and some generous contributions in money
and the materials of war had been received from
strangers, or from the opulent Greeks settled in
some of the chief sea-ports of Europe.

The native Greeks who took the lead in the
Peloponnesus were Peter Mavromikháli, who had
been Bey of *Mani* under the Turks, and Constan-
tine Kolokotróni, who, like his father, had long

E

been a chief of rebellious Peloponnesian Armatolí, and who had held military rank in the Russian and in the English services.

Of the other Greeks who joined the insurrection, the two of greatest note were Demetrius Ypsilanti, who, like his brother Alexander, was an officer in the Russian army, and Alexander Mavrokordáto, member of another of those Greek families of Constantinople upon whom the Porte was accustomed to confer the four great offices of state, held by Christians.* Ypsilanti at first appeared as the agent and deputy of his brother; but the latter, having totally failed in his attempt in the North, Demetrius was soon obliged to give up the high pretensions which he had connected with that character, and as both Hetærists and Russians have since gradually lost their credit in Greece, his influence has declined in proportion. Mavrokordáto was destined to act a more conspicuous and a more useful part.

The capture of *Monemrasía* and *Neó-kastro* or *Navarin* by the insurgents in the beginning of August, 1821, was followed by the investment of *Tripolitza*, of which operation Ypsilanti, by virtue

* Those of governor of Moldavia and of Wallachia, and those of interpreter to the Porte and to the fleet.

of his rank in the Russian service, assumed the
management as far as that was possible among
such a rabble, disobedient even to their native
leaders, and still less likely to submit to a young
man of whom those leaders were jealous.

Tripolitza, situated at the foot of Mount Mænalus on the edge of the plain which contained the
ancient cities of Tegea, Pallantium, and Mantineia,
was surrounded with a slight wall, flanked by towers
at long intervals.   At the south-western end a
small citadel occupies a height, which is connected with the last falls of the mountain.   In the
towers and citadel were about fifty pieces of cannon,
served by a company of artillerymen from Constantinople.   Besides its own population of about
25,000, the town contained the Turkish refugees
of *Londári* with their families, and almost the entire population of *Bardunia*, a part of Mount
Taygetum, which, like *Lalla* near Olympia, had
been colonized by Mohammedan Albanians.   In
addition to the armed men of these several people,
were three or four thousand in the service of
Khurshid Pasha, governor of the *Moréa*, about
half of whom were Albanians.   The command, if
command it could be called, was in the hands of
the kihaya or lieutenant of Khurshid, the pasha

himself having, by order of the Porte, joined the
army before *Ioannina*, leaving his family at *Tripolitza*.

The Greeks at first were very inferior in numbers to their opponents; they had no cavalry;
many of them were scarcely armed, and their besieging artillery consisted only of five or six cannon
and two mortars, wretchedly deficient in their
appurtenances, and managed by a few European
adventurers. Under such circumstances, it is obvious that the best hopes of the Greeks were
founded on cutting off the supplies of the town.
But their opponents had a formidable cavalry,
and few of the Greeks were yet superior to that
innate dread of their late masters, which had made
them, on some late occasions, fly from about one-
tenth of their number of the Turkish horsemen.
At first, collected in irregular bodies under their
several chieftains, they occupied the slopes of
Mount Mænalus. By degrees they approached
nearer to the walls, took advantage of the cover
afforded by the heights near the citadel, placed
their ordnance in battery on the most commanding
parts of the hills, and at length, as their numbers
and confidence increased, they effected a lodgment
in some ruined villages in the plain to the eastward

of the city; and having thus prevented the Turkish cavalry from foraging at a distance from the walls, the distress both of the garrison and inhabitants soon became excessive.

In the middle of September, the besieged were encouraged in their resistance by the intelligence of the arrival of the Turkish fleet, which, after making an unsuccessful attempt upon *Kalamáta*, and, after throwing supplies into *Mothóni* and *Koróni*, had been joined at Patræ by some Algerine ships, as well as by the Kapitána Bay or Commodore, who had been employed on the coast of Epirus against Aly, and who brought a body of Albanians to Patræ. The besieged soon discovered, however, that little hope of succour was to be derived from that quarter, for Ypsilanti having proceeded to occupy the Arcadian passes towards Patræ, no attempt was made from thence to relieve *Tripolitza*, and its investment was never interrupted. One cause of this inactivity on the part of the Turkish commander was the failure of the attempt, which had been made in the early part of the month by their army in Thessaly, to penetrate into Bœotia. They had been met by the insurgents at *Fondána* in the pass of Mount Cnemis, leading from the head of the Maliac gulf into Phocis, and had been obliged to retreat with considerable loss ; no hope remained therefore of any co-operation by the way of the Isthmus.

As the distresses of the besieged increased, so also did the disagreements among their several leaders. Attempts were made to enter into a treaty of capitulation, but the absence of Ypsilanti, and of the Europeans who accompanied him, having put an end to the little resemblance to a regular army, which had before existed, it was impossible to arrange any terms in which the besieged could have the smallest confidence.   From this time there seems to have been an end to all discipline and concert of measures on both sides. The principal men of the city thought only of saving themselves and families, and the Greek chiefs of turning the circumstances to their personal advantage.   The Albanians in the service of Khurshid made a separate agreement for their unmolested return to Albania.   Several rich Turks and Jews purchased the promise of a safe conduct from Kolokotróni and Mavromikháli ; but these, though they received the price of their engagements, were never able to execute them.   On the 5th of October, some of their followers, having discovered what was passing, and being

resolved not to be defrauded of their expected
plunder by the selfish avidity of their leaders,
assaulted the walls on the northern side, and were
speedily followed into the city by all the besieging
forces.

For two days the town was given up to those
horrors formerly common under such circumstances, but which are now happily almost ba-
nished from civilized warfare. That *Tripolitza*
should have been saved from them in the position
as well previous as actual of the contending parties,
it would have been unreasonable to expect. Suffice
it to say, that every kind of excess which a wanton
indulgence in cruelty and a thirst of plunder could
suggest, was inflicted on the Turkish and Jewish
inhabitants of this unhappy place ; and that, when
victims failed within the walls, the Greeks proceeded to put to death a large body of defenceless
inhabitants, who, having been allowed to remove
from the town in consequence of the famine, still
remained in the vicinity.   On the third day after
the assault, the Albanians, who had quitted the
place in safety, which they owed less to the good
faith of the enemy than to the protection of their
arms, departed towards Patræ ; and on the following day the citadel capitulated to Kolokotróni.

Of the hostages who had been received from
different parts of the Peninsula in the spring, two-
thirds had perished by sickness, ill usage, or actual
violence. Although this circumstance may have
increased the sufferings of the captured city, it
cannot be supposed to have had much influence
upon its fate ; this is too well accounted for by the
character of its assailants, a great part of whom
had been robbers or pirates, and whose savage
disposition was neither repressed by any treaty
with the besieged, or by the influence of any civilized individuals of their own nation or of any
other. The Greek chieftains had sufficient power
only to save the harem of the Pasha, together
with the Bey of Corinth, and a few others of the
enemy, whose influence it was thought might be
useful in the sequel.

Both in a military and political point of view,
the capture of *Tripolitza* was a most important
event for the Greeks. It gave them all the interior of the Peninsula, and confined the Osmanlys
to five maritime fortresses. It frustrated the hopes
of the Turkish admiral, furnished arms for several
thousand men, and inspired great confidence in
the ultimate success of the insurrection at a critical
moment. Although it added very little to a better

administration of affairs, and not a dollar to the
national treasury, it enabled the chieftains to keep
their forces united by regular pay, and hence gave
them greater authority in promoting any designs
of utility, as well as greater power for the future
in repressing the cruelty and ill faith which had
disgraced the cause at *Navarin*, as well as at
Tripolitza, and which rendered the acquisition of
the other fortresses in the *Moréa* more difficult,
by obliging the Turkish garrisons to hold out to
the utmost extremity.

Not that we suppose it would have been
possible, by any degree of caution and humanity
on the part of the leaders of the insurrection in the
Peloponnesus, to have prevented by their example
the horrid cruelties which were perpetrated in
other parts of the empire, wherever the unarmed
Greeks were left at the mercy of a large Turkish
population, or wherever the lower orders of Greeks,
in the first intoxication of freedom, and amenable
to no tribunal of their own nation, could find an
opportunity of indulging the vindictive feelings
which for so many ages had been rankling in the
bosoms of their race. These cruelties were the
inevitable consequence of the previous position of

the two people: but the Greeks have been im-
mensely the losers in the sad account of misery
and slaughter; for the insurgents, having been
reduced to the desperate necessity of pursuing the
main object of their liberation without any regard
to the fatal effects which it might have on their
brethren more exposed than themselves to Turkish
vengeance, the result has been, that while all the
numerous Greek families, inhabiting the maritime
districts, or the great towns of the European and
Anatolian divisions of the empire, have been and
still are entirely at the mercy of their oppressors;
it has been only in some parts of Northern Greece
and the *Morèa*, or in a few of the islands, or in
the incursions of the islanders on the coast of Asia,
or on being intercepted at sea by the Greek ships
on their return from the Levant in the first year
of the war, that the Turks have been exposed to
cruel treatment from the Greeks.   The Turks of
Greece were few in number; they were armed,
they resided chiefly in fortified places, or they had
it in their power to retire into the fortresses; so
that, in fact, the Greeks have had little opportunity except at *Tripolitza,* of retaliating upon
the defenceless families of the Turks for the fate

of so many thousand Greek women and children whose mildest lot has been that of being sold for slaves.

We have dwelt upon the proceedings at *Tripolitza* at some length because they give a good idea of the state of the people at the beginning of the insurrection, and shew how totally unprepared the Greeks were, both in a moral and military sense, for the great attempt upon which they had embarked, and the very rashness of which one cannot but admire.

If the savage customs engendered by long subjection to an Oriental yoke appear at this period of the contest in all their deformity, the subsequent history of the insurrection seems to indicate, that they are already giving way to the effects of a consciousness of the dignity of the new position which the people is assuming: it can hardly be doubted, that these sentiments, combined with a better knowledge of regular warfare, which the volunteers from civilized Europe will introduce among them, together with a longer practice of war, which cannot fail to call forth the nobler qualities of the people, will cause the selfishness and cruelty of the robber gradually to give place to a conduct more liberal, and to a more patriotic

and enlightened feeling for the general welfare of
Greece.

By the loss of *Tripolitza*, the Turkish admiral
was obliged to confine his operations to the destruction of *Galaxídhi*, a Greek town which had risen to
considerable opulence by maritime commerce, upon
the site of the ancient Œanthe, in the Crissæan
bay of the gulf of Corinth; and the ships of which
place were prevented from joining the insurgents
in the Ægæan sea, by the enemy's position at the
entrance of the gulf. The Turks burnt the town,
captured thirty or forty Greek ships which were
lying there, and by this operation became undis-
turbed masters of the Corinthian gulf, into which
the Greeks, however strong, can not venture to
pursue them, as long as they remain masters of
Patræ, Naupactus, and of the two intermediate
castles. These castles, called the castles of
the *Moréa* and of *Rúmeli*, stand upon the ancient
promontories of Rhium and Antirrhium, on either
side of a strait a mile in width, and thus command
the entrance of the gulf.

Having left a squadron in possession of the gulf
of Corinth and bay of Patræ, the captain pasha
quitted the latter place in the beginning of October, on his return to the Dardanelles. Near *Zante*

he was met by a great number of Greek vessels, but without any result except the loss of one of his small ships of war, which was stranded and burnt in the port of *Kierí* in that island.

This year the Turks had been surprised: they began the campaign of 1822 better prepared, and with the advantage of having at length obtained possession of the last strong hold of Aly Pasha, whose cause had become almost identified with that of the Greeks.   Khurshid Pasha was now charged with the entire conduct of the war in Greece, and Omér, a Toshke Albanian of *Ver-ghiondí*, near *Beráti*, (and hence commonly called Omer Vrionis) who had distinguished himself in the service of the Viceroy of Egypt, particularly against the English at Rosetta, in 1807, received the pashalik of *Ioannina* and *Arta*, in the room Ismaïl, as a reward for having set the example of treachery towards his late master Aly, by opening the passes of Pindus to Ismaïl on his first advance to *Ioannina*, in 1820.   The exhibition of Aly's head at the imperial gate, in February, 1822, and the triumphal conveyance into the capital of a part of his spoils, excited a degree of enthusiasm very useful to the cause of the sultan at an important moment: but a small part only of the pasha's gold

reached the imperial treasury, while the substitu-
tion of one Albanian for another in the government
of *Ioannina* showed how completely the Greek
insurrection had thwarted the design of the Porte
for increasing its authority in Epirus; affairs
having in fact become less favourable to the future
influence of the Porte over Albania, than they
had been under Aly, or than they would have
been under the government of his sons.

Nevertheless the spring of 1822 was the crisis
of Grecian liberty, and its cause appeared to many
persons little better than desperate. On one side
was a power larger in extent of territory than any
in Europe; which had maintained its station for
near four centuries, in one of the most commanding positions in the world; whose integrity was
admitted by all the other great powers to be essential to the general peace; ready, by the nature
of its government, to enter upon war at a short
notice, and furnished with all the fiscal, military,
and naval establishments of a monarchy of long
standing. On the other, were the inhabitants of
a small province of this extensive empire, without
any central authority, without cavalry, artillery,
magazines, hospitals, or military chest, whose
whole military force, in short, consisted only of a

rude undisciplined infantry, armed with an awk-
ward long musket, to which was added, according
to the circumstances of the individual, pistols, a
dagger, or a sword—ignorant of the use of the
bayonet, acknowledging no discipline, and more
uninstructed in war as an art than the Greeks of
the heroic ages,—led, indeed, by men possessing
courage and enterprize, and some of the essential
qualifications of command, but who were scarcely
less ignorant and unenlightened than their soldiers, and too selfish to lose any opportunity of
enriching themselves, or to preserve that harmony
with the other leading men, which was so necessary in the dangerous position of the country.

There were circumstances, however, which
rendered the inequality between the two parties
more apparent than real, and there were others
which, although more distant perhaps in their
effects, are so powerful, that they will probably
have the effect of excluding the Turks from the
Peloponnesus for ever, and may even ultimately
expel them from Europe.

Among the former may be reckoned the degeneracy of the present race of Turks as soldiers;
the ignorance and inexperience of their commanders, often raised from situations the least fitted

to give military knov ledge; the total want of
subordinate staff officers, or of officers of any
kind qualified for the conduct of a campaign;
their deficiency in any organized system of supplies in the field; the corruption of the government in every gradation; and, though last, not
least, the poverty of the Porte, which has long
disabled it from supporting a corps of Janissaries
much greater than is necessary for the garrisons
of the empire: thus leaving an army in the field
to depend principally for its numbers upon the
followers of the provincial governors, added to
the feudal and local militia who, from ancient
custom, are exempted from keeping the field between November and May, and who never fail to
return home in the winter. And hence it has
occurred that, for many years past, the Porte has
been unable, except perhaps on the northern
frontier, where are the principal garrisons of the
Janissaries, to keep together an army of 10,000
men for more than six months, or even for a
shorter time, unless when plunder is immediately
in view.*   So great, nevertheless, are the re-

* In the winters of 1799 and 1800, the army of the Grand
Vizier in Syria was reduced to less than 5000, but on entering Egypt in 1800 and 1801, there were not less than 40 or

sources of such an extensive empire as Turkey in supplying its yearly losses, and in thus enabling the government to repeat its attacks indefinitely, that its deficiencies might not have much affected the final result against a people more unprovided than themselves, had not that people been a Christian nation, and situated on the borders of Christian Europe, where religious sympathy, although it may not have been very warmly felt at first, must at length be excited as the contest proceeds, and from whence assistance will, at first secretly, and at last openly, be afforded to struggling fellow-Christians, until public opinion throughout Europe shall identify the success of the insurrection with the cause of Christianity itself.

While the Greeks show a remarkable quickness in adopting the improvements of European art and science, of which we have a striking ex-

50,000 collected. We have seen what clouds of Asiatic Turks were instantly collected by the plunder of Chios. It may be asked how have the Russians been prevented of late years from marching to Constantinople. But the northern frontier, as we have just observed, is an exception, and although the Turks have ceased to distinguish themselves in a regular campaign, it is evident that a people among whom every man is armed, and animated by religious as well as national hatred, may still offer a formidable resistance to the advance of an enemy through their own country.

F

ample in the use they have already made of
fireships; the Turks, whose patriotism chiefly
shows itself in bigotry and the persecution of
all other religions, and whose government, however desirous, has always found it impossible to
give the necessary encouragement and protection
to Europeans willing to assist them with their
military skill, will be left to its own exertions,
and the precarious aid of the Musulman powers
of Africa.

It is obvious that a contest between two people
such as we have just described cannot resemble
war as it is carried on between two of the civilized
nations of Europe, equally practised in the art of
war, and equally provided with its materials. A
people possessing only an irregular infantry cannot meet cavalry and artillery in the plains, but
however adventurous they may be, are of necessity reduced to a defensive war in their own
mountains. In like manner, the merchant brigs
and polaccas of the Greeks, though well manned
and skilfully conducted, cannot be expected to
place themselves alongside the two-decked ships
and frigates of the Turks. Many persons who
have not considered these circumstances have
ascribed to a want of courage and enterprize on

the part of the Greeks, that which has been the inevitable consequence of the military position and resources of the two people.

In the beginning of 1822, the Greeks had already begun to feel the benefit of some of their advantages; the good wishes and good offices of the people of Europe were shown by meetings in various countries to assist the cause with officers, ammunition, and money, while the unanimity which the hope of liberty and a single year of successful insurrection had excited in the nation itself was no less manifested by the assemblage of deputies from every part of insurgent Greece, who, having met at *Piadha,* in the Epidauria, on the 1st January, 1822, promulgated their independence, and instituted a provisional constitution.

Two circumstances also occurred at this time, very encouraging to the Greeks and to their well-wishers in Europe, though neither of them was destined to give any permanent advantage to the cause. One was the hostilities which had broken out on the Persian frontier of Turkey, and which at least gave the Turks of the eastern part of Asia Minor an excuse, always readily seized by them, for keeping their contingents at home. The other was, the surrender of the Acro-Corinthus, one of

the fortresses which had been constructed by the
Venetians when in possession of the *Moréa;* and
a point which will be of the utmost importance to
the protection of the peninsula, when the Greeks
know how to make use of it.

But the immediate cause of their successful
resistance in the campaign of 1822 is to be found
in the peculiar nature of the country; in the suffi-
ciency of the Greek troops to the defence of their
mountains against an enemy who had no infantry
of a similar kind, except that of Albania, which
was chiefly confined to western Greece; in the un-
fitness of cavalry alone, and especially such irregular and undisciplined cavalry as that of the
Turks, to retain the country which it overran,
and to keep up the communication between the
districts to the southward of Mount Œta and
the positions in Thessaly, where alone they had
any magazine; but, above all, it was derived from
the great defensive strength of the approaches to
the Peloponnesus, as well as from that of the
peninsula itself, when assisted by such a naval
force as obliges the enemy to make his principal
attack by land through the Isthmus.

And here it may be necessary to define the
meaning of the chorographical expressions which

we shall have occasion to employ in describing the proceedings of the two contending parties.

In terms most general, Greece may be divided into Insular, Peninsular, and Continental, or, in other words, the Islands, the Peloponnesus, and Northern Greece. The last of these may be subdivided into Greece to the South and to the North of Mount Œta, the latter containing Epirus, Thessaly, and Macedonia, and including also the modern subdivision of *Albania*, the whole of which is comprehended in the ancient Epirus, or within the most extended limits of Macedonia.

But the division of Greece, political and military, which has been adoped by the Greek government, is that of the Islands, the Moréa, Eastern Greece, and Western Greece; of the two latter the great ridge of Pindus forms the separation: for this range of mountains runs from north to south through the whole extent of Northern Greece, dividing it longitudinally into two unequal parts, (the eastern being the greater,) and terminating in the Corinthian gulph, between Naupactus and the Crissæan bay.

The defensive strength of the Peloponnesus by land does not in the present circumstances consist in its isthmus, which, being formed of low land, four miles in breadth, offers no means of resisting

very superior numbers, without a large regular
army, and such assistance from art as is totally
out of the power of the Greeks. In the hands of
such troops as theirs, the great protection of the
Moréa from the northward lies in that double
barrier of mountains which separates the isthmus
from Bœotia; the first of these, anciently known
by the names of the Oneia and Gerenia, lies between the Isthmus and the plain of Megara; the
second, under the ancient names of Cithæron and
Parnes, stretches from the Corinthian to the Euboic gulf. Athens lies between the two lines,
but it is separated by such strong defiles from the
Megaris, that it may be doubted whether the
direct route from Bœotia into the Megaris across
Cithæron, or the circuitous route through the
passes of Mount Parnes and the Eleusinia is the
more difficult, in the presence of an active enemy;
and there is scarcely a third choice, for the approach along the steep shore of the gulph of
Corinth is of the most hazardous kind, particularly on the cornice of Cithæron, between Creusis
and Ægosthenæ, the difficulties of which route are
illustrated on two occasions in the Hellenics of
Xenophon.*

---

* l. v. c. 4.   l. vi. c. 4.

The Bœotian plains terminate to the north-west in the valley of Phocis and Doris, watered by the Cephissus and its branches, which have their origin in Mount Œta. This valley separates Mount Parnassus from a prolongation of Œta, anciently known by the names of Callidromus and Cnemis, the northern face of which looks down on the valley of Spercheius and the Maliac gulf, where some hot sources issuing into the maritime marshes at the foot of the steepest part of Mount Callidromus gave name to the celebrated pass of Thermopylæ. The valley of the Spercheius extends thirty miles westward into the interior; to the north it is separated from the great plains of Thessaly by a branch of Mount Othrys, whieh stretches eastward to the Pagasetic or Pelasgic gulf, and towards the west is connected with the mountains of Dolopia, and through them with Mount Pindus, and the barriers which separate Eastern from Western Greece.

As Callidromus is immediately connected with the highest summits of Œta, which mountain extends quite across the continent to the Ambracic gulf and to the coast of Acarnania, it was impossible for the Turks to dislodge the insurgents, unless momentarily, from their positions in Cnemis

and Callidromus ; but, on the other hand, as the
Turks possessed the post of *Zitúni*, (the ancient
Lamia,) situated at the important point where the
road from Thessaly, through the branch of Othrys
just mentioned emerges into the valley of the Spercheius over against Thermopylæ, there remained
no positions capable of offering any impediment
to the Ottoman forces between the north of Thessaly and the barriers of the Megaris, except those of
Callidromus and Cnemis, which contain the passes
leading from the valley of the Spercheius into that
of the Cephissus.   As to Thermopylæ itself, it is
no longer of the same importance as in the time
of the Persian, or even of the Gallic invasion of
Greece, the new land formed at the mouth of the
Spercheius having rendered it easy in summer,
for an army provided with means for crossing the
river, to turn the pass to the eastward.   This
had been actually done by the Turkish army in
September, 1821, just before their defeat in the
passes of Mount Cnemis.

As a position of great strength in itself, however, and as a central point for observing the
enemy in the Maliac district, and for occupying
the passes of the Callidromus, with a view to in-
terrupt his communication between Thessaly and

Bœotia, and to harass his advance or retreat, Thermopylæ is a post of the first importance, and, as such, it has, from the beginning, been occupied by the Greeks.

In Western Greece, which we have already designated as the country lying westward of the crest of Mount Pindus, there is a series of plains and vallies lying between that mountain and a parallel, though very irregular, range which borders the entire extent of the western and southern coasts of Northern Greece, from the Acroceraunian promontory to the Isthmus of Corinth. These vallies, although separated from each other by some difficult passes, constitute a natural chain of communication from Macedonia and Illyricum, as far as the coast at the entrance of the Corinthian gulf. Proceeding from north to south, these vallies are as follows—the maritime plain in which were the ancient cities of Dyrrhachium and Apollonia—the plain of *Kórytza*—the valleys of the branches of the Aous above the Fauces Antigonenses, containing the modern towns of *Premédi*, *Arghyró-kastro*, and *Kónitza*—the plains of *Ioannina*—of *Arta*—and of *Vrakhóri*. The last of these, which lies below the ruins of Stratus and Thermus, and contains the Lake Trichonis, is

watered on the western side by the *Aspro*, anciently the Achelous.   It is separated only by an
abrupt ridge from the narrow maritime district of
Calydon, in which is the modern *Mesolonghi*, and
by a similar barrier from that of Naupactus, which
is still a fortified town and harbour, called *Épakto*
by the Greeks and *Lepanto* by the Italians.   The
most remarkable interruption in this line of communication through Western Greece is caused
by the Ambracic gulf, which divides Epirus from
Acarnania ; at its eastern extremity rises a steep
woody mountain, now called *Makrinóro*, which
formerly separated Amphilochia from the Ambraciotis, and which constitutes a pass of great
strength and importance, corresponding to that of
Thermopylæ at the eastern end of the Œtæan
range ; for these mountains, as we have already
remarked, stretch quite across the great isthmus
lying between the Maliac and Ambracic gulfs;
and, as they form a continuous mass with Pindus,
as well as with the mountains on the northern
shore of the Corinthian gulf, they complete the
barrier between Eastern and Western Greece,
and render the communication between them in
every part a military operation of extreme difficulty.

As long, however, as the Turks possess the fortified towns of Patræ and Naupactus, and the castles on the Capes Rhium and Antirrhium, they are, by means of an adequate naval force, masters of the navigation of the gulf of Corinth, and may transport across it any troops collected on the Ætolian shore opposite to Patræ or on any part of the northern coast of the gulf, for the purpose of co-operating with an army destined to enter the Peloponnesus from Eastern Greece by the Isthmus.

This great advantage formed the basis of the plan of campaign arranged at Constantinople for the year 1822.   The recent conquest of *Ioannina* had placed in the hands of the Turks the strongest and most important point in Western Greece; *Prévyza* gave them a ready communication with their fleet, *Arta* the command of the whole level on the northern side of the Ambracic gulf; while *Vónitza** assured to them a safe pas-

---

* *Arta*, the ancient Ambracia, stands on a strong height in the midst of one of the most fertile plains in Greece, on the left bank of the Arachthus, about six miles from the mouth of that river in the Ambracic gulf, now called the gulf of *Arta*. *Prévyza* is in the district of Nicopolis; it is situated over

sage into Acarnania. At these points it was
hoped that an army of Albanians would speedily
be collected, sufficient to reduce the whole country
as far as the entrance of the gulf of Corinth, before the army of Eastern Greece could arrive at
the Isthmus. Meantime the fleet of the Capitan
Pasha was to collect troops from the coast of
Asia, and to proceed to Nauplia, which had been
invested during the whole winter by the Greeks;
after having relieved that place and opened a
naval communication with the army of Eastern
Greece, which it was calculated would by that
time have entered the *Moréa*, the fleet was to
proceed to Patræ, where they were to debark
another body of troops, and then to transport into
the *Moréa* the forces of Albania and Western
Greece, which, after quelling the insurrection in
Acarnania and Ætolia, were to be collected on

against the site of Actium, on a peninsula on the northern
side of the narrow strait which leads from the Ionian Sea
into the bay of Anactorium.   A second strait unites the
bay of Anactorium with that beautiful little inland sea, the
Ambracic gulf.   *Vónitza* is situated in the district of Anactorium, but within the second strait at the south western extremity of the Ambracic gulf.   Of these three important places,
Prevyza, which was fortified by Aly Pasha, is the only one of
any strength.

the opposite coast by the pashas of *Ioannina* and *Épakto*.

The particular circumstances, which deranged the Turkish plan of operations, were, 1. the continuance of the war in Epirus. The Suliotes, who had been replaced in possession of their impregnable castle by Aly Pasha, encouraged a spirit of insurrection among the Christian inhabitants of the mountains surrounding the plains of *Ioannina* and *Arta*, which, by alarming the Turks for their communication through the passes separating these two plains, confined their attention to the northern side of the Ambracic gulf, and gave time to their adversaries to prepare for making head against them. Mavrokordáto, president of the Greek Executive Council, finding that all the real power in the *Moréa* was in the hands of the military chiefs, and sensible that the peninsula could hardly be saved, unless the war were maintained in Western Greece, persuaded his colleagues to consent to his assuming the chief direction of affairs in this quarter, where he had already acquired some experience and influence in the preceding year, while Aly was defending himself in *Ioannina*. His views were chiefly directed to the Armatolí of the great tract of moun-

tains lying between Thessaly and the south-western
coast, who form the chief strength of the insurrection in Greece beyond the Isthmus, as well as
to the great defensive resources which the nature
of that country affords against an enemy from
Epirus. He derived some ultimate hopes also
from the effects of that doubtful attachment to
the Porte, and from those divisions between the
Mohammedans and Christians in Albania, which
would probably increase as the contest proceeded.

Mavrokordáto arrived at *Mesolonghi* in May
with a corps of European foreigners, about 100
in number, styled Filéllenes,—a Greek regiment
called regular, of 600 men, commanded by a Piedmontese, a small body of Suliotes under Marko
Bótzari, and a few other Armatolí. His first
object was the relief of *Suli*, in which he was assisted by a body of Maniátes under the brother
of Mavromikháli, who were landed at Port *Fanári*
near *Parga*, the ancient Glykys Limen. But Mavrokordáto, having been ill seconded by some of
the chieftains of Western Greece, had only collected 2000 men, when, after having crossed Ætolia, Acarnania, and Amphilochia, he took post at
Kombóti, near the opening from the pass of *Makrinóro* into the plain of *Arta*. From this posi-

tion, in which the Greeks successfully resisted
some attacks from the Turkish cavalry, they proceeded to *Peta*, a strong hill near *Arta*, to which
there is only one access from the plain, and which
being connected with the mountains separating
the Ambraciotis from the Molossic plains which
surround the modern *Ioannina*, furnished the rea-
diest means of cutting off the intercourse of the
enemy through the strong passes on the road
from *Arta* to *Ioannina*, as well as of establishing
a communication with *Suli*. But a check which
Bótzari received in his advance towards *Suli*, and
the treachery of a captain of Armatolí from Athamania,* to whom the key of the position of *Peta*
was entrusted, ruined all their hopes. In the
midst of a general attack from the Turco-Alba-
nian forces at *Arta*, this coward or traitor fled to
the mountains and left the Filéllenes, after a gal-
lant resistance, to be cut to pieces or taken prisoners by the Turks. About the same time the
entrance of the Turkish army into the *Moréa* and
the arrival of the Capitan Pasha's fleet on the

---

* The Athamanes, one of the 'Ηπειρώτικα ἔθνη, occupied the
vallies of the Arachthus, and the mountainous country lying
between the Ambraciotis and the great summits of Pindus to
the N.E.

western coast of Greece having given the worst
aspect to the success of the insurrection, Mavrokordáto was obliged to abandon, for the present,
all attempts to the north of the Ambracic gulf.
It was not long before the news of the result of the
invasion of the peninsula by land, together with the
retreat of the Turkish fleet from the western coast,
restored some hopes to the cause in Western
Greece; but the leader of the Maniátes having
been slain near Suli, and the Suliotes having been
reduced to the utmost distress, they were under the
necessity in September of accepting the British
mediation, and, giving up the castle of Kiáfa to the
enemy, they were transported to Kefalonía.   Mavrokordáto preserved for some time his positions
in Acarnania; but the defection of another of
the captains of Armatolí obliged him at length
to give up all the country westward of the
Achelous; and in the beginning of November,
after some attempts to defend the strong approaches to the Ætolian lagoons, his followers
were invested by land and sea in the peninsula of
Mesolonghi and in the island of *Anatolikó*, whose
inhabitants retired into the adjacent islands or the
Peloponnesus.   These places were inaccessible
from the sea except by shallow boats; on the

land side the isthmus of *Mesolonghi* was defended
by a single low wall and a ditch. To this the
besieged added an interior intrenchment, connect-
ing two churches; their artillery amounted to five
or six small pieces, and there were not 500 fight-
ing men in the place. Notwithstanding this
wretched state of preparation, they resisted for a
fortnight the attempts of a large body of Osmanlys under Reshid Pasha, the fire of several 24
pounders and howitzers, and the more formidable
activity of the Albanians, in the service of Omér
Pasha of *Ioannina*, when some Greek ships, having
raised the naval blockade, and brought reinforcements and supplies from the Peloponnesus, the
patience of the Osmanlys became exhausted, and
hostilities were less actively pursued. After the
failure of a general attack, for which the Turks
chose as usual a Greek festival, (the night of
Christmas or of the 5th of January, 1823,) the
intelligence which the besiegers received, of a
large body of the Moreites, under Mavromikháli,
having landed in Acarnania, alarmed them so
much for their retreat across that province, threatened as they already were by the Armatolí, collected on all the mountains in their rear, that
they made a sudden retreat through the passes of

G

Mount *Zygós* to *Vrakhóri,* leaving ten or twelve
pieces of cannon and a great part of their camp in
the hands of the enemy. The Turkish cavalry
saved the infantry from being attacked in the
plains; but the wintry terrors of the Achelous,
and an enemy hanging upon them on every side,
exposed the Albanians to considerable loss in
their retreat through Acarnania, and Omér Pasha
reached *Vónitza* with a very small number of followers.

2. The second immediate cause of the failure
of the Turks in the campaign of 1822, was the
insurrection of Chios, which was excited by a small
party in that island in conjunction with the Samians.   Although nothing could be more imprudent than this enterprize, or more contrary to the
wishes of the great majority of the numerous inhabitants; for the island, at the same time that it
owed its prosperity to its commerce with Asia and
Constantinople, had no adequate means of defence
against the fleet or the Turks of the adjacent
coast of Ionia—although the rash and cruel
attempt was in its consequences so disastrous to
the peaceful community, that it would be difficult
to find the parallel of their sufferings any where
but in ancient history ; the event, it must be con-

THE GREEK REVOLUTION. 83

fessed, was extremely useful to the cause of Grecian independence, by rendering accommodation more difficult, and by adding to the other motives of exertion a general conviction among the Greeks, that there was no safety but in the success of their arms. It was fatal to the Turkish plan of campaign, by detaining the fleet and the Asiatic troops on the coast of Asia; thus preventing their intended co-operation with the armies in Eastern and Western Greece: at the same time that it led to another event of great importance, which, besides causing further delay, tended powerfully to establish the character and confidence of the Greek islanders. On the 18th of June two boats, manned by some seaman of *Psará* entered the canal of Chios with two fire-vessels, which at night they attached to the two largest ships of the Turks. One of these escaped without much damage, but the admiral's ship was burnt, and the Capitan Pasha himself was killed by the fall of a mast in endeavouring to reach the shore with the very small portion of the ship's company which escaped destruction. So great was the effect of this exploit, in confirming the fears which the Turks already entertained of the Greek fire-ships, that they did

not dare to venture into the narrow extremity of
the Argolic gulf, either in proceeding to Patræ or
in returning from thence, although in the former
instance the success of their army, which was then
entering the *Moréa*, depended upon it, and in the
latter case the saving of the fortress of Nauplia
from capture.

3. A third cause which prevented the Turks
from executing a combination of operations in
this campaign, was the impossibility of maintaining
a constant communication between Eastern and
Western Greece, through the mountain-barrier
which separates them. The most frequented passage is that which takes its name from the modern
town of *Métzovo*. It crosses a central ridge of
Pindus, on one side of which are the fountains of
the Arachthus, flowing into the Ambracic gulf,
and on the other those of the Peneus, which, after
traversing the Thessalian plains, flow through the
pass of Tempe into the gulf of Thessalonica.
This road, in crossing the mountain from west to
east, quits the Molossic plain near *Ioannina*, and
on the opposite side of Pindus descends upon the
site of Æginium, now occupied by the town of
Staghí, or *Kalabáka*, situated on the edge of

the plain of Upper Thessaly, which formerly contained Tricca, Gomphi, and some other large cities. Although the easiest of all the passes, which communicate between Eastern and Western Greece, this route presents great resources for defence, and although free from danger as long as the castle of *Ioannina* and the person of Aly were the main objects of the Porte, it was frequently interrupted by the Armatolí from the country of the ancient Æthices, Athamanes, and other rude tribes of Epirus and Mount Pindus, after the war had become more general, and the insurrection of the Greeks had assumed a consistency. The passes lying farther south, which lead from the plain of Upper Thessaly through Athamania, into the Ambraciotis, or through Dolopia and the Ætolian mountains into the plains bordering upon the lower part of the Achelous, were still less practicable. In the course of the summer, a large body of Turkish cavalry was severely punished for their rash attempt to penetrate in the former direction to *Arta*, through the defiles leading from the site of Gomphi. The Turks were met by a body of Armatolí at the bridge of *Koráki*, on the Achelous, and were so completely defeated, that

it was with difficulty that a small part of them
effected a retreat into the Thessalian plain.*

Thus, by the effect of these several causes, the
main body of the Ottoman army assembled in the
plain of Larissa, was left to its own unassisted
exertions in its attack upon the Peloponnesus by
the way of the Isthmus.

It was towards the end of May, 1822, that
Khurshid Pasha, having failed in some attempts
on *Suli,* and having finally resigned the conduct
of the war in Western Greece into the hands of
the Albanian Omér, now Pasha of *Ioannina,*
joined the army at Larissa in Thessaly. His
forces were principally collected from Rumili.
There were about thirty thousand troops of the
Porte, more than a third of whom were cavalry;
and there were ten or twelve thousand horse of
the Ayans, or great feudatories of Rumili, besides
the personal guards of the respective pashas.†

* In the year B.C. 189, Philip, son of Demetrius, King of
Macedonia, followed the same route in his expedition against
Amynander, King of the Athamanes : he met with equal difficulties, and the result was exactly similar.   See Livy, l. xxxviii.
c. 2.

† It is so extremely difficult to arrive at numerical accuracy
in Turkey that we have seldom ventured to state the numbers

The month of June had entirely elapsed before the preparations for advancing beyond the Spercheius were considered by Khurshid as complete.

No sooner had he given the order for advancing, than the cavalry which formed the largest, or at least by far the most efficient, part of his army, leaving the artillery and infantry far behind, crossed the ridges of Othrys and Œta without opposition. The former was hardly defensible, as the important points of Pharsalus, Thaumaci and Lamia were in the hands of the Turks; but it was expected that Thermopylæ and the passes of Mounts Callidromus and Cnemis, which were then occupied by Odhysséfs (Ulysses) son of Andrisko, a native of the neighbouring Doris, who had been captain of the Armatolí of all this part of the country under Aly Pasha, and who had so successfully opposed a large army of Turks at the same spot in the preceding year, would have presented a vigorous resistance. Whether the inactivity of Od-

---

on either side in this war. The present estimate rests on the authority of a physician in the service of Khurshid, who was present when the Pasha stationed himself with the other Turkish leaders for three days on the side of the bridge of the Spercheius, near Thermopylæ, while the army defiled over the bridge.

hysséfs on this occasion arose from a spirit of
opposition to the central government, with which he
had had some recent disagreement, or whether he
calculated, that by allowing the enemy to spread
over a larger tract of country, the Greeks would
have it in their power to intercept his communications, and to harass him in detail with better effect,
for which object the nature of the country and
other circumstances were so admirably adapted,
is perhaps known only to Odhysséfs himself.
His courage and ability had hitherto been emi-
nently useful to the cause of his country.   He
soon afterwards opposed Khurshid himself at the
head of the reserve of the Turkish army with
success; he has since repeatedly shown how
formidable a barrier to the South of Greece, the
Œtæan passes are in his hands : and whatever
may have been his motives upon this occasion,
the consequences of his conduct, although at first
alarming, were ultimately most beneficial to the
Greeks.

The Turkish army having crossed Phocis and
Bœotia, plundering, burning, and murdering,
while they published the amnesty of the Porte,
arrived at Corinth, without having met with any
resistance in the mountainous barriers of the

Megaris—and this proof of discord or debility in the Greek councils was followed by another still stronger in the surrender of the Acro-Corinthus, which the Greeks had neglected, or, to speak more justly perhaps, had been unable, from a want of means, to supply with ammunition, engineers, or provisions.

Elated by such an important capture, the Turks advanced in full security to occupy the Argolic plain, and to open a communication with the garrison of Nauplia which had already, in the end of June, agreed to deliver up the place if they should not be relieved in forty days.*

As soon as the enemy entered the Argolis, the Greek government gave up the entire management

---

* A few days earlier, the Acropolis of Athens had surrendered to the Greeks, after a siege protracted to a great length by the want of means on the part of the besiegers. After the surrender, when the Turks were waiting the arrival of European vessels to transport them into Asia, according to the terms of the capitulation, the Athenians, or their allies, alarmed at the approach of the Turkish army, attacked their prisoners in violation of their engagements, and put about half of them to death. The Athenians then took refuge for a second time in Salamis. It ought perhaps to be mentioned, as some palliation for this inhuman and faithless act, that the Greeks of Athens had been cruelly persecuted by the Turks, when Omér Vrioni occupied Athens in the preceding autumn.

of the contest to Demetrius Ypsilanti, to Mavromikháli and Kolokotróni, and embarked on board
their ships in the Argolic gulf. Ypsilanti with a
small force occupied the ruined castle which stands
on the site of Larissa, the ancient citadel of Argos.
The two other leaders collected together the
Armatolí of the Peloponnesus.

The Turkish army was commanded by Mehmet
Pasha of *Drama* (the ancient Drabescus) in Macedonia, who occupied all the eastern part of the
Argolic plain with his troops, and entered Nauplia.
Here ended his progress. In vain he looked for
the Turkish fleet, as well to furnish the supplies
which the devoured country around and in his
rear could no longer afford, as to assist his movements by the debarkation of a body of troops on
the Lernæan side of the plain of Argos, without
which operation on the enemy's flank he soon perceived that it would be difficult for him to penetrate any farther into the peninsula ; for besides
the defensive resources which the Greeks found in
the town of Argos, there was a still stronger position in their rear behind the Erasinus, a river which,
issuing from under a steep mountain, connected
with the ridges of Arcadia, which were then occupied by the Greeks, crosses a marshy plain to the

sea near Lerne: beyond this important line of defence again were the rugged passes of Hysiæ and Mount Parthenium, which separate the Argolic plain from the Tegeatis or plain of *Tripolitza*.

Without cavalry, artillery, or much concert among themselves, the Greeks maintained their ground for several days in the ruined houses of Argos, or in the vineyards along the banks of the Inachus, where they protected themselves against the Turkish cavalry behind entrenchments and excavations. When driven out of these positions by the fire of the Turkish artillery, to which they had nothing of the same kind to oppose, they still maintained a successful resistance on the Erasinus, and behind the rocks and ruined walls of the hill of Larissa.

While every day increased their numbers in the surrounding mountains, a total want of provisions for men and horses soon rendered it impossible for the Turkish commander to continue in his position, or any longer to delay his retreat into the Corinthia. There is no outlet from the plain of Argos in the direction of Corinth, but through the passes of *Barbáti* and *Dervenáki*, which lead from either side of the ancient Mycenæ into the valley of

Cleonæ, and from thence through another pass into the maritime plain which includes Sicyon, Corinth, and the Isthmus. Some of the Turks effected their retreat towards Corinth, and one body threw themselves under the protection of the guns of Nauplia, but the greater part fell victims, on the 6th and 7th of August, to their own indiscipline, and to the improvidence and rashness of their leader, in the passes of Tretus and Mount Eubœa, on either side of the ruins of Mycenæ, where a Grecian imagination might picture the ghosts of the Atridæ witnessing, from their still existing sepulchres, a slaughter of the barbarian hosts, from which Greece may perhaps date her resurrection from slavery; for, in fact, this was the most important event that had yet occurred during the contest.

On the 18th and 19th August, the Ottoman commander, after having received reinforcements and pressing orders from the Seraskier, made attempts to regain the Argolis; but the Greeks having occupied the passes of the Corinthia in their rear, as well as having resisted them in front, they were at last obliged to fight for a safe retreat into the plain of Corinth.

In the meantime the Greek senate had sent some

ships round to the port of Cenchreæ to occupy the Isthmus, and Odhysséfs had filled the barriers of the Megaris with his Armatolí, so that the Turks, defeated as they were, had no longer any retreat from their positions at Nauplia and Corinth. They were sufficiently strong, however, to maintain themselves in these two places during the autumn, and it required all the vigilance of Kolokotróni to prevent their communication. At length, on the night of the 12th of December, the garrison of the *Palamídhi*, or upper fort of Nauplia, reduced to despair by famine, quitted that post, and retired into the lower fortress, when the Greeks, who were investing the place, having perceived what had happened, occupied the *Palamídhi*, and the garrison of the town surrendered upon condition of being transported in safety into Asia.

This was the most valuable capture the insurgents had yet made, as, together with a harbour in the most conveninent of all situations for an intercourse between the peninsula and the islands, it gave them the fortifications and public buildings erected here at a vast expense by the Venetians, when they made this place the seat of their government in the *Moréa*. Another event of still greater benefit perhaps to the Greek cause, which

occurred about the same time, was an order issued
by the British government to their officers in the
Mediterranean acknowledging the right of the
Greeks to blockade the ports of Greece which
remained in possession of the Turks. Though
adopted in conformity with the observance on the
part of Great Britain of a strict neutrality between
the two contending parties, it was regarded by the
Greeks as a first step to the recognition of their
independence in the most important of all quarters,
at the same time that, by giving them a prospect
of depriving the Turkish garrisons of a great part
of those supplies which had been a very profitable
object of speculation to some persons in the Ionian
islands and elsewhere, it afforded them a hope of
effecting such a blockade as might lead to the
reduction of the enemy's fortresses in the Peloponnesus, in the only manner which the want of
military resources seemed as yet to admit of.

The remaining operations of the Turkish fleet
in the campaign of 1822 were still more inglorious
than those which have been related. The Porte
entertained hopes that, notwithstanding the long
detention of the fleet on the coast of Asia, its co-
operation might still be useful in the *Morea*.
Without making any attempt to relieve Nauplia,

the fleet proceeded to Patræ, took on board at
that place the officer who was appointed to fill the
post of Capitan Pasha, disembarked a small body
of troops, but entirely failed in the main object of
the expedition.   The insurrection in Western
Greece, although not very successful, had been
sufficient to occupy all the Albanian and Ottoman
forces collected in that quarter.   The new admiral
was unable even to effect a communication through
Achaia with the army of Eastern Greece in the
Argolis; and that army was defeated, and its
remains, in two separate bodies, had taken shelter
under the guns of Nauplia and Corinth, before the
admiral had sailed from Patræ for the eastern
coast of the peninsula.   It is obvious that the
march of the army ought to have been arrested so
soon as it was known that a delay had occurred in
the departure of the fleet from the Asiatic coast:
but once set in motion its progress could no longer
be stopt; the troops had been carried forward by
the necessity of seeking new supplies, until they
were collected in the Argolis without the power of
advancing, and long before the fleet, destined as it
was to make a previous visit to Patræ, could possibly
reach the Argolic gulf. It was not until September,
when little was left for the fleet to perform but the

relief of Nauplia, that it arrived near *Spetzia* at
the entrance of the Argolic gulf, where it was met
by a great number of the insurgent vessels. The
Greeks, unable to use their fire-ships in the open
sea, did not venture to approach the heavy artillery of the Turks, who, on their part, would not
expose themselves to the Greek fire-ships in the
narrow extremity of the gulf near Nauplia. Instead
of entering it, therefore, the Turkish admiral sent
in two vessels, which were intercepted by the
enemy before they could reach Nauplia: he then
sailed to Crete, and from thence to Tenedos,
where in the middle of November he was attacked
at anchor by the same enterprising Psarian, Con-
stantine Kanáris, who had burnt the former Capitan Pasha's ship at Chios, and with similar success.
On this occasion, however, it was the Capitan Pasha
who escaped and his comrade who suffered. After
some further losses from the weather, the remaining Turkish vessels sought safety in the Dardanelles, and thus ignominiously closed the naval
campaign of 1822.

The second congress which met at *Astró*, in the
ancient Thyreatis, on the maritime frontier of
Argolis and Laconia, in the month of April, 1823,
found that a year had made a great increase in

public confidence and in the extent of the insurrection, while the recent advantages obtained
over the enemy gave the best hopes for the future.
Their military position in general, however, was
nearly the same as in the preceding year. The
Turks were still in possession of all the fortresses
of the *Moréa* except two, with just so much of the
level country of Northern Greece as their posts
at Larissa, Lamia, and the Euripus could command. In other respects their embarrassments
were increasing: the Porte found great difficulty
in equipping its fleet, and had resorted to such
violent measures for sustaining its finances, that
the piastre, which not many years before had been
equivalent to an English shilling, was now reduced
to the forty-fifth part of the pound sterling.

But, on the other hand, the wealth of the commercial islands and towns of Greece were equally
exhausted by the exertions which had been made
since the beginning of the contest; some of the
powers of continental Europe continued to regard
the insurrection as part of a general conspiracy
against established governments; the others re-
fused all countenance to the insurgents; and individual charity was very inadequate to supply the
wants of a people in the situation of the Greeks.

H

Hence they were unable to retain in their service
or to satisfy even the most moderate expectations
of the numerous military men of experience, who
had been left in idleness in every part of Europe
by the general peace, and who were anxious for
employment in Greece. They were unable even to
take into the service of government their own private ships by which all their naval efforts had been
made, or to execute the repairs of a two years war for
them: so that the number of those ships in a state
to oppose the enemy was considerably diminished.
Still less could they organize an artillery or create
a corps of infantry under the orders and in the
pay of the executive, without which it was impossible for the government to follow any improved
plan of military operations, or even to establish a
national treasury, collect the taxes, and administer,
for the benefit of the revenue, all that large portion of the property of the insurgent districts,
which, having formerly belonged to the Turks or
their government, was now confiscated to the
state.

A government without a treasury, a marine, or
an army, was of course little better than a cypher:
nor was it in the power of the deputies assembled
at *Astró* to confer the authority that was wanted.

The acts of this Congress, therefore, were little more than a repetition or revisal of those of the preceding year. They once more issued a formal assertion of independence, made some amendments in the provisional constitution, and again authorized the executive to borrow money upon the security of the public revenue. The collecting of the contributions in every part of Greece, except the islands, and with it all real power, still remained in the hands of the illiterate chieftains of the land forces, who, though brave and sincere in the cause, were too ignorant to see the necessity of giving way to others for the general advantage: some of them feeling no inclination to submit to an abridgment of their power or their profits, and all of them being naturally more disposed to trust to themselves for obtaining the resources necessary to keep their followers together, than to a government in which they could not possibly have any great confidence. And thus the Congress, although, by the numerous attendance of deputies, it furnished an useful evidence of the improvement of the cause of independence in extent, consistency, and unanimity of purpose, left the affairs of the country in the same

anarchical state in which it had found them. The
two military chiefs of greatest influence, Mavromikháli and Kolokotróni were made President
and Vice-President of the ἐκτελεστικόν or Executive Council, and having thus both the civil and
military powers in their hands, they reduced the
senate, or βουλευτικὸν σῶμα, to total imbecility.
The latter attempted, indeed, to preserve its authority, and was engaged during the remainder
of the year in endeavouring to check the abuses
of the military government; but two successive
presidents, Kundurióti and Mavrokordáto, having
fled to *Ydra*, the remaining members, after frus-
trating an attempt of the party of Kolokotróni to
seize the archives of the senate at Argos, retired
to *Kranídhi*, at the extremity of the Argolic peninsula, near *Spetzia*. Here they speedily elected
a new executive, at the head of which was placed
the Ydriote Kundurióti. And thus the party of
the naval, or insular leaders of the insurrection,
was in open hostility with that composed of the
military chieftans and of some of the primates of
the Peloponnesus. Nothing can more strongly
show the perfect similarity of the modern Greek
character with that of the ancient people, than
these dissensions in the midst of the most immi-

nent danger; and that they have not interrupted a spirited defensive resistance to the enemies of their national independence and religion.

As the military situation of the two parties had not materially altered, the Ottoman plan of campaign was nearly the same as in the former year, and the chief difficulty in its execution was again caused by the immense strength of the country. As before, the great object of the Porte was to effect a simultaneous attack upon the northern coast of the *Moréa* from Eastern and from Western Greece, by means of their fleet and of the positions which the Turkish forces preserved at the entrance of the gulf of Corinth. But it was proposed in 1823, to make the maritime command of the gulf more useful, and to establish a better concert of operations between Eastern and Western Greece. Instead of a sudden incursion into the Peloponnesus, the Ottoman forces were not to attempt the passes of Cithæron and the Megaris until they had pushed forward detachments from the Bœoto-Phocic plains to occupy the bays of Crissa and Anticyra (now called the bays of *Galaxídhi* and *Aspraspítia*), and the port of Creusis (*Livadostro*). A large corps of Albanians under Mustafá Pasha of Scodra was to assemble at Tricca, now called *Trikkala,* with the view of effecting a junction in the plain of the Achelous with the other Albanian forces collected at *Arta* and *Prévyza* under Omér Pasha of *Ioannina,* and after having taken or masqued *Mesolonghi* they were to cross over into the *Moréa,* reinforced by the Asiatic troops which were to be brought to Patræ by the Capitan Pasha's fleet. The part of the army of Eastern Greece which was to be assembled in the ports on the northern shore of the Corinthian gulf, was to be transported across the gulf into Achaia, and to clear the road along the Achaian coast, where, as the land rises immediately from the shore into high mountains, connected with those of Arcadia, it is difficult to maintain an uninterrupted communication by land from Patræ to Corinth without a large force.* The united army would then raise the blockade of the Acrocorinthus, and would be in readiness to act in concert with the remainder of the army

---

* The division of the Turkish army which retreated to Corinth after the defeat in Argolis, in August, 1822, attempted, after the fall of Nauplia in the ensuing January, to make their way to Patræ, but were met by the Armatolí of Nikíta and some other chiefs in the maritime passes of Ægeira and Ægæ, and, with the exception of a party of Albanians, who capitulated upon conditions, were all either slain or made prisoners.

of Eastern Greece, collected in the plains of Bœotia; the Megaric barriers of the Isthmus would
be simultaneously assailed on both sides, and a
junction would be effected without any loss. It
was undoubtedly an improvement upon the plan
of the preceding year. To the Albanians, who
are alone fitted to contend with the Greeks in
their native mountains, was left the difficult task
of subduing Acarnania and Ætolia, while the
main Osmanly army, assembled in the eastern
plains of Thessaly, reinforced by a corps which
was to be landed by the Capitan Pasha at the
Euripus before he sailed for Patræ, would, it was
calculated, occupy without difficulty, all the country to the foot of Mount Cithæron.

But the defects in the Turkish system, which
have already been developed to the reader, were
more than sufficient to render totally unsuccessful
a plan, the complete success of which would have
required a much larger army than the Porte has
for many years been able to collect, together with
an accuracy of combination which none but the
most efficient government can command. In the
naval department the Ottomans received more
effectual succour than in the preceding year, from
the Barbary States, especially the Algerines,

whose ships and seamen were much better adapted
than their own to contend with the Greeks; the
latter being, moreover, as we have already observed, less strong at sea than they had been in
the two former years. With all his exertions,
however, the Capitan Pasha was unable to reach
Patræ before midsummer, after having effected
a junction with the Barbary squadron in the
month of April, after having detached reinforcements to Crete, and landed supplies at Volo,* as
well as at the fortresses of *Kárysto* and *Égripo* in
Eubœa, and of *Koróni* and *Mothóni* in Messenia.

The insurrection, which had now become very
formidable along the range of Olympus, Ossa,
Pelion, and Othrys, threatened the rear of the
Turkish Army in Thessaly too much to admit of
a large force being sent into Bœotia, until Pelion,
at least, had been reduced. That mountain being
the most formidable position of the insurgents,
from its numerous population, its peninsular
strength, its easy communication with the Greek
naval forces, and its central situation in the chain
of the eastern range of mountains, was very judi-

---

* A Turkish castle situated in the plain at the head of the
Pelasgic gulf, between the sites of Pagasæ and Demetrias.

ciously the chief object of the Turkish commander ; but the town of *Tríkhiri* and the promontory of Mount Tisæum on which it is situated,
on the eastern side of the entrance into the Pelasgic gulf, affords such an excellent point of
retreat to the Magnesian insurgents, that the
Turks, although they obtained some temporary
success, were unable to produce any such result
as could materially assist the general plan of the
campaign.

In like manner, although a body of Ottoman
troops from Thessaly, joining that of Eubœa,
overran Bœotia and Attica, and even entered the
town (but not the citadel) of Athens, the Armatolí
of Odhysséfs, and other chieftains, were sufficient
to prevent them from approaching the Isthmus,
or even from occupying any of the ports on the
shore of the Corinthian gulf, having made them
pay dearly for all their attempts to penetrate
through the strong passes of Helicon and Parnassus.

In the autumn the Turks found themselves
under the necessity of withdrawing a part of their
forces into Thessaly, while with the remainder
they cruelly persecuted and plundered the inhabitants of Eubœa, who the less deserved it, as

they had hitherto been slow in joining the insurrection. The Osmanlys, however, were soon
followed into this island by Odhysséfs, who
having been speedily joined by some of the Armatolí of the Thessalian mountains, and assisted
by reinforcements landed from the Greek fleet,
forced the enemy before the winter to retreat
behind the walls of Carystus, and of the Euripus.

In Western Greece the Armatolí of the great
continuous ranges of Pindus and Œta, under
Sturnári, Ysko, and other experienced captains,
maintained a communication across the continent
from Epirus to Mount Pelion and Eubœa, in spite
of their formidable Albanian opponents, who
occupied the country around Tricca.   Several
partial endeavours were made to penetrate the
Greek line of defence during the early summer,
but it was not until the arrival in the month of
July of Mustafá Pasha of Scodra, (for upon this
modern Gentius and his Illyrians all the remaining hopes of the Porte for the campaign now
rested,) that a serious attempt was made to effect
the object of passing from the plains of Upper
Thessaly through the Dolopian and Ætolian
mountains into the plain of *Vrakhóri*, for the purpose of there effecting a junction with the troops

of Western Greece which were collected in the districts of Ambracia and Anactorium.

The Porte, always justly doubtful of the fidelity of the Albanians, had given the direction of the latter part of the expedition, that which was collected in the Ambracic gulf, to the Osmanly Yussuf, of *Serres* (Sirræ) in Macedonia, commander of the Turkish positions and forces at the entrance of the gulf of Corinth; a preference which gave so much offence, as well as alarm, perhaps, for his own head to the Albanian Omér Pasha, that he is supposed to have encouraged the defection of a large body of Albanians, which took place at *Vónitza* in the beginning of August, at the momont when Yussuf was about to march from thence with his army through the passes of Acarnania. The Albanian deserters passed round the gulf and through the *Makrinóro*, without any molestation from the Greeks, with whom they were probably in correspondence, and Yussuf Pasha was so much alarmed at the event, that he immediately returned to Patræ, leaving the prosecution of affairs in Acarnania in the hands of Omér.

Not long afterwards the army of the Scodrian met with a disaster of a different kind. Having

crossed the ridge of *Agrafa,* and taken post near
Karpenísi, a town situated at the foot of Mount
Velúkhi, (the ancient Tymphrestus, which separates the waters running to the Spercheius from
those which form a branch of the Achelous,) they
were attacked by the Greeks in the night of the
21st of August and defeated with great slaughter,
and the subsequent plunder of their camp. The
numerical loss of the Greeks was very trifling,
but the victory was dearly bought with the life of
the heroic Marko Bótzari, who had penetrated
with a chosen body of Suliotes into the centre of
the enemy's position. Notwithstanding these
checks, however, the two Albanian leaders succeeded in surmounting all the efforts of the Armatolí to oppose them in the passes of the Ætolian
and Acarnanian mountains, and having at length,
in the end of September, effected a junction in
the Ætolian plain on the left bank of the Achelous, they speedily established a communication
with Patræ, Naupactus, and the squadron which
had been left on the coast by the Capitan Pasha
on his departure for the Ægæan. They then
penetrated through the passes of the lake Trichonis, and the defiles of Mount Aracynthus,
which form the last of the strong defences of

the maritime plains and lagoons lying between the
Achelous and Evenus, and *Mesolonghi* was once
more threatened with a siege.   But the failure of
every other part of the plan of campaign rendered
fruitless the exertions of the two Albanian chiefs;
the Ottoman forces had retreated from Bœotia
into Thessaly and Eubœa, and the Acro-Corinthus surrendered to the Greeks in the middle of
October; Mustafá of Scodra, therefore, after
having ineffectually bombarded *Anatolikó*, and
made an unsuccessful attempt to convey troops
into that island in boats, began his retreat in November towards the north of Albania; Omér
Pasha once more retired to his positions on the
Ambracic gulf: and Mavrokordáto returning,
about the same time, to his government with
a small squadron from Hydra and Spetzia, Mesolonghi was relieved for the present from its naval
blockade.

The Turkish admiral, in returning to the Hellespont, was met, at the end of September, near
Mount Athos, and again at Sciathus, by Miaoúlis
the Ydriote, with a squadron of Greek ships, and
sustained some damage, together with the loss of
one of his small ships of war.   A convoy proceeding from Thessalonica to the Euripus was about

the same time attacked by the Greeks, and suffered great loss, in the bay of Opus on the Locrian
coast. But the Turks had avoided any disasters
such as those of the preceding year, by leaving
their great ships at home, and by trusting chiefly
to frigates, which being more manageable, and
offering less temptation to the attack of the
enemy's fire-ships, were at the same time too hea-
vily armed to be approached by the small Greek
vessels. The Greek navarchs, however, had not
been deficient in their usual activity, having
effected debarkations on the coasts of Asia Minor
and of Macedonia, which, although they exposed
the Greeks in the Pergamenian district and in the
Macedonian plains to a cruel persecution, were
extremely useful to the general cause in Greece;
while the former detained the Turkish forces in
Asia, the expeditions to the Macedonian coast
were equally useful in preventing the Pasha of
Salonika from reinforcing the army in Thessaly;
for it may be here observed, that the advantages
which the physical structure of the country has
given to the insurrection are in no part of Greece
more remarkable than in the great Macedonian
or Thracian peninsula of Chalcidice, which termi-
nates in the three small peninsulas of Pallene,

Sithonia, and Acte, or Athos. These strong positions of the insurgents, open to their insular friends by sea, pressed on one side upon the great plains of Lower Macedonia; while on the other there was an insurrection extending through the whole Olympian range as far north as the mountains of Edessa and Pella, so that the Pasha of *Salonika* has from the beginning of the revolution found ample employment for all his disposable force. The Osmanlys, being very strong in his province, had indeed been enabled in November, 1821, to force the intrenched position of the Greeks at Cassandria or Potidæa on the Isthmus of Pallene, and to satisfy their thirst of spoil and vengeance in that Peninsula. They exercised similar cruelties on taking *Naussa*, a town in Mount Bermius on the past of the Olympian ridge between Berrhæa and Edessa in the spring of 1822, but the insurgents, assisted by some of the Armatolí of other parts of Greece, and occasionally by the fleet, were never long prevented from keeping up a resistance along the whole eastern side of Greece, from the extremities of Athos and Pallene, and from the northern frontier of Proper Macedonia through Olympus, Ossa, and Pelion, to Œta, Pindus, and the western coast of Greece.

Among the larger islands, Samos and Crete have been the only two seriously engaged in the war. In Crete, the Sfakiotes, like the Maniates of the *Moréa*, formed the basis of the insurrection, and by means of the assistance which they received from the insurgent government, the Cretans were enabled to maintain the war with tolerable success during the two first years, under the Ydriote Tombazi, who was sent to assist them with some ships, and to conduct their operations; but the very large proportion of the Musulman population in this island, aided by the ships and troops sent in two successive summers by the Pasha of Egypt, has lately been too powerful for the declining means of the Greek government; and the Cretan insurgents have now been obliged to retire into the mountains, and a few maritime positions.

The strength of the old Venetian fortresses of *Candia, Canea, Retymo,* and *Suda,* will probably enable the Turks to maintain those posts as long as the Ottoman fleet can traverse the Ægæan, and, perhaps, long after they have lost all the rest of the island.

Samos has from the beginning of the contest set an example to the important islands of the Asiatic coast, which the latter, not containing, like Samos, a population entirely Christian, nor possessing so defensible a country, have shewn little readiness to follow. The Samians, on the contrary, instead of being deterred by their proximity to the Asiatic continent, from which they are separated by a strait only a mile broad in the narrowest part, have taken advantage of this circumstance to make frequent landings in Ionia, and have even extended their ravages to a considerable distance in the valley of the Mæander. These incursions, like those of the Psarians on the coast of Æolis and of the northern part of Ionia, although often disgraced by cruelty, have been a most useful diversion to the cause in Europe, by detaining the Osmanlys in Asia; and hence, from the beginning of the contest, it has been considered an object of the first necessity with the Turks to effect the reduction of Samos and *Psará*. Several ineffectual attempts have been made against Samos; and it is the main object of the naval campaign of the present summer to attack in succession all the strong holds of the insurgents in the Ægæan with the allied fleet of the Moham-

I

medan powers, having on board a numerous body of troops of debarkation, consisting largely of Albanians. The event of these attempts, most formidable, it must be confessed, to such small communities, is not yet known: but it may safely be anticipated, that whatever footing the Turks may gain in the summer will be lost in the ensuing winter; and, moreover, that it will not be obtained without great sacrifices, for it is next to impossible for the Turkish ships to leave their harbours without suffering from the elements, from their own unskilfulness, or from the superior seamanship and enterprise of their opponents. Even when the only object of their summer excursions was to collect the tribute from the islands and *Mani*, they seldom reached Constantinople on their return without having suffered considerable damage from their want of skill alone.

The following is the Turkish plan of campaign by land for the present year (1824)—20,000 Albanians under Mustafá Pasha of Scodra to march through *Ioannina* and *Arta* upon *Mesolónghi;* 10,000 Albanians under Omér Pasha to cross Mount Pindus into Eastern Greece, and to march upon Athens; 20,000 men under Dervish Pasha to march from Larissa by *Zitúni* upon

Sálona (Amphissa) and the Crissæan bay of the
gulf of Corinth; the army of Yussuf Pasha, commander of the forces at the entrance of the gulf
of Corinth, to be reinforced by 10,000 Janissaries,
who are to be disembarked there from the fleet
of the Capitan Pasha; and finally, the army of
Egypt, commanded by Ibrahim Pasha, son of the
viceroy Mohammed Aly, to proceed with the
Egyptian fleet to the *Morêa.* Thus we have the
same intentions as in the preceding year, the
same lines of movement, and, with the exception
of the Seraskier at Larissa—the same commanders. The only addition is the Egyptian
army; and we are told that a formidable expedition against Greece is in preparation at Alexandria. But the Viceroy of Egypt, although, as
a Musulman, by no means indifferent to the
Sultan's cause, nor so independent as to disregard
the consequences of being a declared rebel, cannot consider the Greek war as vitally affecting
his interests. It must be admitted that the history of his life proves him to have great ambition
as well as talents; and it is impossible to foresee
the extent and duration of efforts which depend
upon the views or passions of an individual; it
may be presumed, however, that he will not easily

I 2

part with the best or largest portion of those
troops upon whom his own safety depends ; for a
Turkish satrap has always an enemy in the Porte,
and is never exempt from the apprehensions of
treachery and revolt. As to the other parts of the
Turkish scheme of operations, it would not be very
rash to prognosticate, that so many as 10,000
men will not be collected upon any one of the
points of assembly indicated : that Omér Pasha,
at once fearful of the Porte, of the Scodrian chieftain, of a formidable rival, who threatens his here-
ditary possessions in middle Albania, and of the
Albanian chieftains in Epirus, who were united
with the Greeks in support of Aly, and who have
never acted cordially with the Turkish government, will not move far from his own capital; that
if the Greeks in Western Greece are tolerably
united, it will be still less in the power of the
Scodrian to take *Mesolónghi* than it was in the
last year; and that in Eastern Greece the amount
of the Turkish exploits will probably be to over-
run the plains of Thessaly and Bœotia with their
cavalry, and to devour the harvest, if the desolation of the two preceding years has left any labourers to cultivate the fields.

Having thus laid before the reader a sketch of

the previous condition of the Greeks, together with the leading facts of the insurrection, he will be enabled to exercise his own judgment, on the probabilities of the final result. It has been seen that, while the insurgents have been increasing in confidence and numbers, have obtained some of the fortified places, have caused the destruction of many of the enemy's ships, and have had the superiority over them in the field on some important occasions, the latter have not gained a single advantage, that can serve as a step towards subduing the insurrection. Such has been the termination of a three years' contest between the small vessels of some of the most skilful seamen in the world, against large ships, ill manned, and conducted by ignorance and inexperience—between cavalry and artillery against infantry, in a country peculiarly formed to give importance to the latter.

But if the existence alone of such an insurrection for so long a period as four years is sufficient to prove that it never can be suppressed without foreign assistance; on the other hand, the excessive ignorance of the Greeks in the art of war, their want of union, and their poverty, still leave them far removed from that complete possession of the country, which can alone authorize them to

insist upon an acknowledgment of their independence, either by their Turkish adversaries or by
other nations. Before they are qualified to hold
this language, they must, above all things, be
masters of the fortresses of the *Moréa*. The great
importance of Patræ and Naupactus, with the
naval command of the gulf of Corinth, which
depends upon them, has already been exemplified.
The destiny of Eastern Greece is no less dependent upon that of *Égripo*, the only place of
strength in the hands of the Turks to the southward of Thessalonica : for *Zitúni* and *Volo* are
feeble garrisons, exposed to be cut off by the
insurgents in Pelion, Othrys, and Œta, whenever
the Osmanlys are not in force in the plains on
either side of them.

Égripo, a corruption of Euripus, occupies the
site of the ancient Chalcis, and is connected by a
bridge of about 100 feet in length with the Bœotian shore of the strait, from which rises a commanding hill occupied by the Turkish fortress of *Karabá-
ba ;* and hence it is not sufficient, in order to invest
Égripo, that the Greeks should have possession of
the island of Eubœa, or that they should be able
to prevent the Turkish fleet from relieving *Égripo*
by sea ; they must also be masters of the range

of mountains anciently called Hypatus, Ptoum, Messapium, and Cyrtone, which are united by the chain of Cnemis and Callidromus with Mount Œta, and which contain the passes leading from the shore of the Euboic strait into the plains of Thebes and of the lake Copais.

If the fortress of the Euripus should be taken, the future incursions of the Turkish cavalry into the country southward of Mount Œta would be perilous, and could only be transitory; and as the Greeks would then surround the basin of Thessaly in greater force, and would possess themselves of Tempe and of the strong passes of Mount Olympus, which separate Thessaly from Macedonia, it would probably follow, that the Turks, having no place in the former province capable of any resistance, would be under the necessity of retreating into the plains of Lower Macedonia at the head of the Thermaic gulf, unless they could secure their right flank by means of the Albanians. But enough has already been stated to shew, that in consequence of the mutual dislike existing between the Albanians and the Osmanlys, and of the domestic spirit of dissention in Albania, the Porte, although it may continue to employ the mercenary services of the warlike people of that

country in every part of the empire, cannot depend
much upon the efforts of Albania, as an united
nation, against the Greeks, and that the cause of
Grecian independence, at least to the southward
of Mount Œta and the Ambracic gulf, will not
long suffer very seriously from the vicinity of the
Albanians. It is probable that Albania will gradually relapse into the barbarous state of internal
discord, but national independence, which has been
more or less its condition, as far back as we can
trace its history ; which in times of general danger
may unite its discordant districts under the person
of greatest influence or military talent, as happened in the war of George Kastrióti of Kroya,
(Scanderbeg) against Sultan Mahomet the Second,
but which, at other times, leaves its neighbours
more to apprehend from individual rapacity or
from the incursions of robbers, than from the
united strength or ambition of the nation.

As long as the Turks can preserve the Euripus
and the fortresses of the *Moréa,* especially those
which give them the command of the Corinthian
gulf, they will not cease to entertain a hope of
regaining their ground in Greece, and they will
consequently make every effort to relieve those
fortresses by sea and land, as well as to retain the

occupation of the plains of Eastern Greece, without which they are sensible that the Euripus will not long remain in their possession. The Greeks, on the other hand, are equally convinced of the necessity of making some effort to besiege the maritime fortresses, as the prospect of reducing them by famine must be very precarious as long as they have it not in their power to prevent the large ships of the several Musulman powers from occasionally relieving them. Nothing can more strongly shew the inefficiency of the military government of Greece, than that a post so contemptible as the castle of Patræ should have held out for three years after its investment by the Peloponnesian Armatolí. The want of a treasury has hitherto been the insuperable obstacle to improvements in the conduct both of their civil and of their military affairs; but as private liberality, and the still more effectual aid of the loan, which the pecuniary plethora of England has enabled the Greek agents to raise in London, have removed this impediment to melioration, it may be hoped that the execution of the requisite measures will no longer depend upon any ignorant or rapacious chief of Armatolí who may happen to have a large number of followers. The Greek privateers, which have hitherto so

ably prosecuted the naval war, will be taken into
the service of the state, and a few vessels of a
larger class will be procured: an artillery will be
formed, as well as a regular infantry, instructed in
the European discipline ; and the Armatolí may be
organized as a provincial militia under the ablest
and most trustworthy of their chiefs.   Naupactus
and Patræ will probably be reduced, which must
be speedily followed by the fall of the castles of
Rhium and Antirhium : the Greeks may then
easily keep exclusive possession of the navigation
of the gulf of Corinth, and they may then, but not
before, consider themselves masters of the Peloponnesus.

   To ensure the safety of their conquest, it would
be a most useful measure to form an intrenched
camp extending from the Acro-Corinthus to Lechæum, on the gulf of Corinth, and from the same
citadel to Cenchreæ, on the Æginetan gulf.   The
latter is a line of six miles ; but being occupied by
a steep wall of rock, rising from the south side of
the Isthmus, through which there are only two
narrow passages, the fortifying of this entrance
into the peninsula is not more difficult than that
between Lechæum and the Acro-Corinthus, which
is only two miles in breadth.   With such a fortifi-

cation; with the Armatolí in possession of the
mountains of the Megaris in its front; with all the
harbours of the two gulfs of the "bimaris Corin-
thus" occupied by their vessels, the insurgents, if
they continue to preserve the same spirit which has
hitherto animated them, will be in a condition to
defy the efforts of an enemy, who is unable to
take the field or the sea before May, or to keep
them beyond October. They will then have the
best right not only to treat with their late oppressors on the basis of an acknowledgment of the
independence of a large portion of Greece, but
even to hope for the assistance of some of the
great Christian powers in obtaining it.

Next to the gulf of Corinth that of Ambracia is
the naval position of the greatest importance to the
Greeks. The command of this mediterranean is
of vital utility to their cause, whether for the
defence of Ætolia and Acarnania, and under their
cover for the protection of the Peloponnesus, or
with the more extended view of liberating Epirus
from the Musulman yoke. If the Osmanlys were
expelled from the gulf of Corinth, the insurgents
would be able immediately to turn their attention
to that of Ambracia, and would soon oblige the
Musulman Albanians to evacuate the castle of

Vónitza. Their future progress would be greatly
assisted by building small vessels on the southern
shore of the gulf, where the woods and sheltered
coves furnish great facilities for such an undertaking; they would then be able to cope with the
vessels of the enemy at *Prévyza,* where the depth
of water prevents any that draw more than twelve
feet of water from entering; and they might thus
at least be masters of the Ambracian gulf within
the strait of Anactorium. For any objects to the
northward of the gulf the possession of the fortified and strongly situated post of *Prévyza* seems
indispensibly necessary, as this place commands
the exterior entrance of the gulf, shelters the
Turkish vessels from pursuit from the open sea,
carries on all the maritime intercourse of the south
of Epirus, and is the harbour by which alone the
army of the Northern Albanians can maintain a
communication with their own ports, and receive
their supplies when they advance into Ætolia.
The possession of *Prévyza* would be an important
step to the recovery of *Suli* and the capture of
Arta, upon which will probably depend the insurrection of the Epirote Christians, in the populous
mountain-districts of *Djumérka,* *Zagóri,* and
Pogóyani, as well as in those on the western side

of the plains of *Ioannina.* Should the Moslem Albanians be obliged to retreat from *Ioannina* within the frontiers of Proper Albania, and those of the maritime part of Epirus remain neutral, no part of the plains of Thessaly would be any longer tenable by the Osmanlys.

During the last two years the Porte has been sufficiently alive to the difficulties of its situation to try the effects of conciliation with its rebellious subjects. The Turkish admirals have endeavoured to enter into terms with the three islands which form the heart of the insurrection; and the government has made some spirited efforts to punish or suppress the vindictive spirit of their Musulman subjects in those parts of Europe and Asia where the Greeks, regardless of what they have already suffered, or of the example of their more prudent countrymen who have retired to Samos, Crete, and other islands, are, by the small proportion of their numbers, left at the mercy of the Turks.

In the campaign of last year (1823), besides proclaiming an amnesty, the Porte sent several dignitaries of the Greek church to persuade their countrymen to submission: some of these proceeded from the head-quarters of the Seraskier,

in Upper Thessaly, into the neighbouring mountains: others made a similar attempt in the Peloponnesus; it is almost unnecessary to add, without
the smallest success. For such must be the result
of their negociations as long as the Turks persist
in using the word ' amnesty' only. No one who
has a correct idea of the previous condition of
the two people, who considers to what an extreme
their mutual hostility has now proceeded, or who is
aware of the weakness of the Turkish government,
and how incapable it is of insuring protection to
the Christians, will suppose it possible that the
Greeks can trust to any compact with their late
rulers but such as shall be guaranteed by their
own arms—such as shall liberate them from all
dependence upon Turkish faith and Turkish
mercy—such as shall exclude the Ottomans from
all real authority in Greece.

It might be supposed that the Porte, after the
experience of the three past years, would be not
unwilling to amputate the deceased limb, lest the
malady should spread to more vital parts—lest
a cry of liberty, raised by the entire Christian
population of European Turkey, should be re-
echoed by that of Syria and Armenia; and that
having still so much to fear from her great north-

ern neighbour, she would be inclined to place the
Greeks in a condition to be of greater use to her
perhaps as allies, than they have ever been as
slaves. The Greeks on their side ought to be
still more anxious to come to terms, for although
it may not be possible for the Turks to reduce
the south of Greece to its former state without
the assistance of dissensions among the Greeks
themselves; yet those dissensions will be greatly
promoted by a deficiency of pecuniary means, as
the Turks are fully aware. The war has already
dissipated all the wealth which a long course of
industry had collected; it may be doubted whether Greece has not already arrived at the extent
of her credit with other nations; while the power
which the united forces of Constantinople and
the African states possess of maintaining a naval
war from year to year, cannot be met without
a continued expense, and may lead to the greatest
distress. Let us hope that the glory of putting
an end to this cruel contest is reserved for that
mediation which has already so successfully diverted the threatened hostilities between Russia
and the Porte, thus preserving the general peace
of Europe and equally consulting the true interests
of Great Britain, and the ultimate advantage of
Greece herself.

We shall not detain the reader with any reflections upon the provisional constitution of Greece,
proclaimed at Epidaurus on the 15-27th of January, 1822.*   It is scarcely possible to reduce these
laws to practice in the present state of the country,
and the scheme is confessedly only provisional,
intended to give place to various amendments
when the independence of Greece is confirmed.
And this perhaps is a fortunate circumstance; for
we cannot compliment the Neo-Hellenic legisla-
tors on having adopted the scheme of a quinque-
partite executive, which experience has so well
shewn to be unsuited to civil government.

Still less are we inclined to occupy our readers
with speculations on the probable consequences
of the revolution of the Greeks, on the future
destinies of the remainder of European Turkey,
or with any reflections on the policy of the leading
powers of Europe, as it may be affected by the
same event.   One or two observations connected
with the subject, however, we shall hazard, as the
Greeks may, perhaps, do well to consider whether
they do not furnish an argument for inducing them

* A Copy of the Constitution, accompanied by a Preface
and translation, was published last year in London.   8vo.
Murray.

to embrace the first reasonable offer of their late oppressors, and rather to insist upon terms of safety than extent of liberated country.

It may be observed that no great degree of power and opulence, or of prosperity in agriculture, commerce, or manufactures, can revisit Greece until its population is very greatly increased; that the Peloponnesus would not be so densely peopled as England, if all the Christians of Continental Greece speaking the Greek language were collected in it; that the Peloponnesus, the Cyclades, Euboea, and Attica would form a state chiefly dependent upon naval defence for its safety, and consequently more easy both to establish and preserve than a larger portion of Greece with a more extensive land frontier; and that such a state, if governed with prudence, would infallibly have the effect of meliorating the condition of all the Greeks who might remain beyond those geographical limits, by affording them a refuge from oppression, or by obliging the Turks to treat them with justice and lenity in order to prevent their emigration. We have included Attica in this imaginary partition of Greece, not so much from the prejudice of ancient recollections, as from the immense importance of the

K

Megaris to the security of the Peloponnesus, and
because Attica, which has an excellent frontier in
Mount Parnes, cannot on the one side be separated from the Megaris and Eleutheris, nor on
the other, as ancient history so clearly shews, from
the island of Euboea, and still less when the latter
follows the fate of the Peloponnesus.* Nor would
a treaty with the Porte for the entire liberation of
the southern part of Greece prevent the mountaineers of Helicon, Parnassus, Œta and Pindus,
of Othrys, Pelion, Ossa and Olympus, or the
inhabitants of some of the islands beyond the
Cyclades, such as Lesbos, Samos, Chios, Rhodes,
and Crete, from entering into a separate treaty
with the Porte on an agreement somewhat different. It is obvious that, either from geographical
position, or from their not having made so great
a progress as the Peloponnesians in expelling the
Mohammedans, these people may not have the
same interests, nor be in a condition to treat with
the Porte upon the same terms. It would seem
that, in the first instance, to require an enlarge-

---

* In a state of these limits, it would be very necessary to
include the important posts of *Mesolonghi*, Antirrhium and
Naupactus, situated on the northern shore of the entrance of
the gulf of Corinth.

ment of the bounds of independent Greece beyond
the smallest extent of territory compatible with
safety, or with the existence of a separate state,
would at least produce delay in that which it is
the interest of the Greeks to hasten by all possible means; for it can hardly be doubted that the
independence of any part of the country would
powerfully promote the immediate improvement
and the ultimate liberation of the remainder; at
the same time that it is, perhaps, in the present
imperfect state of Greek civilization, an indispen-
sable preliminary to the formation of a government
capable of preserving order within, as well as the
customary relations with foreign powers.

There are five classes among the Greeks into
whose hands the direction of affairs must necessarily fall, as they alone are qualified for it by the
education, or the power, or the influence, that are
requisite. These are—1st, The military chiefs;
2dly, The primates, or men of landed or commercial property who possessed power under the
Turkish government; 3dly, The higher clergy;
4thly, The persons engaged in maritime commerce,
and particularly the leading men in the principal
islands; 5thly, The foreign Greeks from Constantinople, or other parts of the Turkish empire,

who have joined the insurrection. We have
arranged these classes according to their extent
of influence in continental Greece, and unhappily
at the same time in the inverse order of their degrees of civilization and fitness for conducting
affairs. It has been shewn that the military chiefs,
who have only been rendered superior to captains
of banditti, by the late increase of their followers,
and by the noble cause in which they are now
engaged, have, by their unwillingness to submit
to the suggestions of more enlightened men, been
the chief impediment to the establishment of
a central government. Several primates have
contributed to the same pernicious result by con-
tinuing to exercise the avarice and meanness which
was the inevitable habit of their lives under the
Turkish government. Among the clergy a *few*
may be found who are among the most enlightened, resolute, and patriotic of the nation; but it
is chiefly upon the fourth class, upon the leading
persons in the commercial and nautical communities of the more opulent islands, who have had
long experience in the art of governing a free
population, and who by their excellent management have contributed to convert barren rocks,
too insignificant to be named in ancient history,

into populous and wealthy republics, that the
friends of Greece would wish to see the task im-
posed of establishing and governing a Greek
state—though without excluding some of the
clergy, primates, and military chiefs, or the more
essential services of the Byzantine or other Greeks
who may be desirous of applying to the use of
the new government the fruits of the education
which they have wholly or partially received in
civilized Europe.

And here we find an additional argument for
confining the first formation of a Greek state to
the islands and provinces which we have just indicated. As such a state would be principally
maritime, its government would more naturally
fall into the hands of that class which we have
just observed to be the most fitted to conduct it.
By avoiding an extensive land-frontier the Greeks
would avoid in a great degree that collision with
the Turks, or with the great powers bordering on
Turkey to the north, which would greatly distract
an infant government, and might retard the establishment of good order. The government would
avoid also the necessity of deferring to the influence of the military chiefs of the mountainous
districts, which form so large a portion of Greece

beyond the Isthmus, in the hands of whom the
more exposed situation of that part of the country would require a larger share of authority to
be placed, and who for a considerable time to
come will probably strive to preserve their military
power, whatever may be the condition of Southern Greece, or in whatever political position the
Northern Greeks may stand towards the government of Constantinople, or towards the Musulmans of Macedonia or Albania.

The sanguine and aspiring temperament, however, which has ever characterized the natives of
this country, has already prompted the insurgents
to look far beyond the Isthmus for the limits of
their independence. Already they speak of including Thessaly within those limits, with the
confident admission that they do not wish for a
more distant boundary. But even in this case it
may be observed by the way, that the northern
frontier of the ancient Thessaly would form a
very insecure boundary, unless it comprehended
also the whole of Mount Olympus. The course
of the river Haliacmon from the sea to its source
in Mount Pindus, which would include a small
part both of lower and upper Macedonia, would
alone furnish a frontier, inclusive of Thessaly,

that would be consistent with safety. This line
might terminate at Mount *Smólika,* one of the
great summits of the Pindus range, near the
Vlakhiote town of *Samarína,* and might be pro-
longed from thence westward so as to include
within the Greek boundary, *Kónitza, Delvináki,*
and *Délvino,* terminating at the cape anciently
called Onchimus, at the northern entrance of the
channel of Corcyra. As this boundary would
place some of the strongest passes of Western
Greece within the Greek line, it would give a good
frontier, where it is most wanted, on the side of
Albania. The middle part of the frontier, having
behind the Haliacmon the range of hills which
connect Pindus with Olympus, and which cover
the western parts of the plains of Thessaly, would
present great defensive advantages as long as the
Greeks could hold their ground in Mount Pindus.
And the eastern part of the line is of immense
strength. The only points of access from Macedonia into Thessaly, on that side, are the pass of
Servia, which leads from the plains of the Haliacmon through the mountains anciently called
Cambunii into the vallies of Perrhæbia, and from
thence into the Pelasgiotis, or plain of Larissa—
the still more difficult pass of Petra, which con-

ducts into the same vallies under the western
side of the great summits of Olympus—and the
succession of strong positions which lie to the
eastward of the same summits, between them and
the sea,* ending in the rocky and (in the face
of an active enemy) the impenetrable defile of
Tempe.

And here it may be remarked incidentally, that
the line which we have just described is precisely
the natural boundary of Modern Greece, if we
determine its limits by language; for in Eastern
Greece the Bulgarian is the prevalent tongue
beyond the Haliacmon, as the Albanian is in
Western Greece beyond the prolongation of the
line of that river, which we have indicated. It is
true that the Albanians have colonized to the
southward of it in the part of Epirus opposite to
Corfú, as far as *Suli* inclusive; but these are
merely Albanian conquests, the language is of modern introduction, and the Greek is equally in use.

* It was in the strongest of these positions, in front of
Dium and behind the river Enipeus, that Perseus resisted
Æmilius Paullus, until Scipio Nasica, with a detachment of
the Roman army, having gained possession of the pass of
Petra, and having thus threatened the enemy's rear, Perseus
retired in haste to Pydna, where the Romans defeated him,
and in one day became masters of Macedonia.

If Thessaly should be excluded from independent Greece on its first establishment, the boundary line might follow up the Spercheius from its mouth in the Maliac gulf to its sources, and from thence nearly along the limits of the ancient Ætolia to *Makrinóro*, or the Amphilochian pass, at the head of the Ambracic gulf. The Spercheius, with Mount Callidromus behind it, forms an admirable frontier; nothing indeed can be stronger, in a military point of view, than the whole mountainous isthmus included between the Ambracic and Maliac gulfs, with the strong passes of Amphilochia and Thermopylæ at the two extremities, especially if the defects created in the latter by the alluvions of the Spercheius were remedied by art; but as a frontier for a treaty of peace, the range of Œta, westward of the sources of the Spercheius, is so blended with that of Pindus, and the inhabitants of all those mountains are so much allied in manners and interests, that it would be very difficult to establish any precise boundary.

Within Mount Œta the only practicable line of frontier for independent Greece, and which, next to the Isthmus of Corinth, is the most marked in Greece, would be that which we have already had

occasion to mention, namely, the crest of the ridge
of Cithæron and Parnes, which forms a distinct
barrier from the Euboic frith to the gulf of Corinth, including within it Attica, together with the
Eleutheris and Megaris.

Although a republic may not be the mode of
government under which a successful insurrection
most speedily settles into good order, as the example of Spanish America has sufficiently shewn,
we must admit that it seems to be the most natural
government for such a country as Greece; that as
physical conformation and geographical position
are the primary causes of the permanent form of
the social system of every nation—thus giving a
limited monarchy to the sea-girt England; a
more military executive to the extensive land-
frontier of France, and a federacy of republics
to the mountains of Switzerland—so a social
compact somewhat similar to that of the latter
country, securing a central authority sufficient
for maintaining the foreign relations of Greece,
and for directing the national security, but leaving much to be executed by the local government of each island or province, appears to be
that which would be the best adapted to the
mountainous intersections, the commercial coasts,

the numerous islands of Greece, and to the great
variety which those peculiarities have caused in
climate, productions, manners, occupations and
interests. The example of ancient history, and
the very general feeling of the people, as shewn in
their almost spontaneous assemblage from the
several islands and districts in congress, seem to
concur in indicating that Greece, if she succeeds
in establishing her liberation, is destined to be a
federative republic. But it cannot be concealed,
at the same time, that this republican tendancy
causes the situation of the people at the present
moment to be still more beset with difficulties
than it would otherwise be, by rendering less
easy that ability to maintain order which must
precede the acknowledgment of their independence by civilized Europe ; for it is to the same
physical peculiarities of the country which have
just been alluded to that we may trace the real
origin of that στασιῶδες and διχόνοια, that spirit
of faction and dissension, which characterized the
ancient Greeks, and which has been conspicuous from the beginning of the present contest,
preventing the exertions of the best men from
having a full effect, suppressing all combination of
useful measures, impeding the formation of a cen-

tral authority, and leaving success to depend upon the rude uncombined exertions of the national will.

But if the Greeks have shewn a want of union as great as that of their ancestors at the time of the Persian invasion, it cannot be denied that the difficulties of their situation are infinitely greater, and that while the contest in which they are engaged is still more truly an ὑπὲρ πάντων ἀγών, than when these words formed part of the song of the Greeks, as they advanced to battle at Salamis,* their previous condition has left them little hope of finding among themselves any of those great characters, which led their ancestors to victory and peace.

Nor, when they shall be relieved from external war, will the arduousness of the great attempt, upon which the people is now engaged, appear diminished on a comparative reference to the situation of ancient Greece. It will not be sufficient for them to form such a divided nation, as, when having successfully resisted in arms the most formidable power with which they were in contact, and mighty in their superiority to all other people in science and the arts, they could indulge in internal emulation, carried to the extreme of

* Æschyl. Pers. v. 405.

hostility. Compared to the rest of Europe, revived Greece will be what the least civilized of its
ancient states was to the whole nation; and such
a federative union as that of the Amphictyonic
council cannot be tolerated in the great republic
of modern Europe.

It has been thought impossible by some persons, that the present generation of Greeks, de-
moralized as they are by their long oriental servitude, should be able to govern themselves. We
shall not be so rash as to hazard a prediction on
this point: it may indeed be reasonably feared,
that the effects of this degradation of character,
repressed in a great measure at present by the
general danger, will be even more conspicuous
when the Greeks are independent. On the other
hand, the necessity of an united government may
go far towards creating it. A community of religion and a constant intercourse with the civilized
world; the increased effect of Christianity, when
no longer in chains, upon the national character;
a church far from adverse to the promotion of
useful knowledge among the people, and much
less superstitious than could have been expected
under its circumstances, — these advantages, in
some of which the modern Greeks are so im-

mensely superior to their ancestors, can hardly
fail to effect a rapid amelioration in their moral
condition.   Already some strong indications of
improvement may be remarked in every class of
the people.   Among the more civilized who are
now attempting to govern the nation, may be perceived an anxiety to merit the good opinion, as
well as to profit by the advice, superior knowledge,
and political experience of those who are more
enlightened than themselves.   Instead of those
unreasonable expectations of an European crusade
in their favour, which many of the Greeks at first
entertained; instead of captious complaints and
unbecoming remonstrances, arising from the want
of a proper sense of their own situation, or from
their ignorance of the history and international
rights of others; further observation seems already
to have convinced the more informed among them
that they ought to be thankful for that neutral
policy, which has left them to depend upon their
own exertions, the only possible road to real independence.   Among the ruder classes, to whose
persevering efforts by sea and land the nation is
indebted for its progress towards freedom, it
would be unreasonable to expect that the traces
of semi-barbarism should at once be obliterated.

As long as their contest continues with an enemy more barbarous than themselves, it cannot be doubted, that we shall occasionally hear complaints of inhumanity and anarchy. On the part of the great majority of their leaders, however, there is a strong desire to arrive at that state of discipline, both civil and military, which can alone correct those irregularities, and save the nation from the disgrace which continues to be not unfrequently inflicted upon it by the faults of individuals.

The further progress of the endeavours of the Greeks to complete their ἀναγέννησις, by entering into the great community of Christian nations, will be chiefly determined by their ability to correct that contentious spirit which is closely allied with their better qualities of industry, enterprize, and genius; and to establish such a state of order among themselves, as shall invite the friendly intercourse of civilized governments, and justify the acknowledgment of their independence. In the mean time they ought cautiously to avoid, in their conduct towards those powers with whom they come into contact, any of that insolence which success or ignorance, or a republican spirit are too apt to generate. It is no less important that they should make every effort to suppress the disposition to piracy, to which the intricate coasts and rocky islands of Greece are naturally liable, and in which some of the more barbarous of the maritime districts often indulged during their subjection to Turkey. To compare this practice, which was marked only by cruelty and rapacity, and the lightest effect of which is a disregard to the maritime laws and customs of the civilized world, with the armed resistance of the mountainous parts of Greece during the long period of Turkish oppression, would be an insult to that which has in fact preserved the last remains of Grecian liberty, during the servitude of the nation. And as maritime irregularities are those which are more immediately liable to give offence to the foreign nations, with whom it is of the utmost moment that the Greeks should be on terms of amity, it should be their most urgent duty to eradicate this vice of the Grecian seas. Above all things they must keep the peace at sea, ʹHMIN γὰρ θαλάσσια ἔργα μεμήλει.

LONDON, *August*, 1824.

THREE or four months have elapsed since the preceding pages were written; the latest intelligence from Greece has brought down the account of military transactions to the season beyond which the Turks are unable to prosecute active operations, and the result of the fourth campaign of the insurrection is ascertained.

By land the situation of the contending parties is not very different from what it was at the close of the first year; but the continuation of an insurrection implies victory to the insurgents, notwithstanding any partial misfortunes to which it may be liable.

In western Greece, we are not surprised to find, from causes which have already been explained, that the Albanian chieftains have made little or no exertions in the cause of the Porte, and that military opertions have been almost suspended in that quarter. During the greater part of the summer Mavrokordáto had his head quarters at *Lygovitzi*, near the western bank of the Achelous, and Omer Vrioni at *Kervasará*, the ancient Limnæa at the south-eastern extremity of the Am-

L

bracic gulf. In eastern Greece, an attempt was
made by the Seraskier Dervish Pasha to penetrate from the plains of Thessaly to the Corinthian gulf, by the route which leads from *Zitúni*
to *Sálona* (Lamia to Amphissa), as an essential
preliminary to the plan of campaign which has
been described. By this movement he would at
once have effected a junction with the Turkish
ships in the gulf, and would thus communicate
with the garrisons which are invested by the
enemy by land at Patræ and Naupactus.

The shortness of the distance from the head of
the Crissæan bay to the Maliac gulf, added to the
facility of maritime intercourse, which the latter
affords with Thessalonica and the Hellespont,
renders the route from *Zitúni* to *Sálona* the most
important passage in Greece next to the Isthmus.
Its military strength is equal to its importance:
and hence all the endeavours of the Turks to
maintain the communication between the gulf of
Corinth and Thessaly by this route have hitherto
been frustrated. It traverses two of the most
remarkable passes in Greece : of these the northern
crosses a ridge which lies between the plain of
the Spercheius and the Dorian valley, near the
sources of the Cephissus, and connects mount

Callidromus with the great summits of Œta: the southern is a narrow defile separating Parnassus from the same mountains.

Of the former of these two passes, the danger was very much diminished to the Turks by their easy access into the valley of Doris, which, by its continuity with the lower valley of the Cephissus, and with the plains of Bœotia, extending to the barriers of the Isthmus, has generally been open to the Turkish troops. But the narrow rocky pass, which leads from *Gavriá*, the ancient Cytinium, into the celebrated plain, which extends from the heights of Amphissa and Delphi to the shore of the Crissæan bay, can never be traversed by them without the greatest danger, while the enemy remains in possession of the mountains on either side of it.

The Seraskier, however, by directing all his efforts to this point, succeeded, in the month of July last, in passing through the defiles; but at *Ampliani*, about eight miles from *Sálona*, he was attacked and defeated by the insurgents, and, after having suffered some further loss in his retreat, he resumed his positions in Doris and in Thessaly, without having effected the smallest advantage to the Ottoman cause.

L 2

In concert with this operation of the Seraskier, an attempt to recover Athens was at the same time made by Omér, a landed proprietor of Euboea, who has been raised by the Porte to the Pashalic of *Égripo*, and entrusted with the conduct of the war on that side of Greece. He was met at Marathon in the middle of July by the Greeks under Goura, where he received such a check as, combined with the ill success of the Seraskier on the side of Locris, has been sufficient to confine his exertions to Boeotia. The latter made an attempt after his retreat from Doris to enter Boeotia to the support of Omér, but met with such opposition in the passes of Mount Cnemis, that he soon gave up the attempt, which was quickly followed by the retreat of the Turks in Boeotia behind the walls of Egripo.

The naval efforts of the Ottoman government have been of a much more formidable character, and the result has been proportionably more glorious to the Greeks, as they have had to oppose all the Musulman powers of the Mediterranean, whose united efforts, if we except the destruction of the two little islands of *Kaso* and *Psará*, have ended in complete failure.

Housref, the Capitan Pasha, after having landed

reinforcements in Eubœa, after having made a
passing attempt to frighten the islands of *Skópelo*
and *Skiátho* into submission, and taken on board
a body of Albanians at Thessalonica, assembled
at *Mytilíni* his armament, amounting to about 150
sail. It is evident that nothing but a combination
of the most determined valour, with the greatest
prudence and good fortune, could enable so small
a community as that of *Psará* to resist such an
overwhelming force. These requisites were in
several respects deficient. On the morning of
the 3d July, a landing was made at the back of
the island while the fleet fired on the town. The
measure was completely successful; the Turks*
quickly drove the enemy's out-posts before them,
and made their appearance on the heights above
the town, when the greater part of the Psarians
retreated in confusion to their ships and put to
sea, in which operation great numbers of them
were lost. The town was then taken, and the
greater part of the remaining population was
massacred. The garrison of one of the fortified
posts destroyed both themselves and the assail-

---

* A great part of these were Albanians. It was by a body
of Musulman Albanians also that Casus was taken in the
middle of June.

ants by setting fire to the powder magazine: the others capitulated. On the arrival of the Psarian refugees at Ydra, Miaoulis sailed to Psará, from whence the Turkish admiral had already withdrawn his armament, and where the Ydriotes found about 1000 Turks and about 20 ships in the harbour. The greater part of these they destroyed, and rescued a part of the ordnance belonging to the island, together with some Psarians who had concealed themselves in the hills. The Greeks then brought away the cannon left in the fortresses; the island has since that time remained desolate: and all its citizens, who have escaped slaughter or slavery, are, like the Athenians in the Persian war, indebted for a refuge to the hospitality of their countrymen in various parts of Greece.

The next operation of the Turkish Admiral, in the prosecution of his design of successively attacking the several strong holds of the insurgents in the islands, was an attempt upon Samos, for which a large body of Asiatic troops was collected at *Skalanóva*, a town in the Ephesian district at the northern entrance of the strait which separates Samos from the Ionian coast. A part of this force, detached to the foot of mount Mycale, was to be transported from Cape Trogilium to the opposite shore, where stood the ancient Samos, while another body from *Skalanóva* was to be debarked on the northern side of the island at *Vathy* and *Karlóvasi*. The Samians sent their families with provisions to the mountains, and remained in readiness to defend the passes, if the Turks should succeed in landing, while a division of the Greek fleet under George Sakhtúri of *Ydra* prepared to oppose the enemy in the straits.

On the 17th August, in a fourth attempt of the Turkish fleet to effect the passage of the strait, the same Kanáris of *Psará*, who had already burnt two Turkish line of battle ships, attached his firevessel to a 40-gun frigate under sail; the fire very speedily reaching the magazine, the greater part of those on board were destroyed, as well as several transports to which the fire communicated. At the same time other fireships burnt a Tunisine brig of war and a large Tripolitan corvette. On the 21st August the fleet of transports employed in carrying over the land forces to the north side of Samos were dispersed, and a part of them taken or destroyed. On the following day the Turkish fleet again attempted to effect the passage from Cape Trogilium, but such was now the

dread of the Greek fireships among the Turks,
that the mere approach of two or three of them
was sufficient to drive back the Ottoman men of
war to the Asiatic coast. The troops, who were
assembled on the shore of Mycale in readiness
to embark, on witnessing this last disgrace of
their navy, returned to the camp at *Skalanóva*, and
it was not long before the greater part of the land
forces, which had been collected at that place,
dispersed and retreated into the interior.

The Capitan Pasha, feeling the necessity of
giving up the attempt upon Samos for the present, proceeded to effect a junction with the
Egyptian expedition at Cos and Halicarnassus.
Sakhtúri in like manner united his force with that
of the chief navarch Miaoulis, at Patmos, after
which the Greeks proceeded to observe the Musulman armament. On the 5th September a
small division of Greek vessels with two fireships
approached the Turkish fleet, when the latter got
under weigh; the Greek fleet then joined their
comrades, and an action taking place, the Turks
lost some men, and two fireships of their opponents exploded without having done any damage
to the enemy. The Greeks then retired to Pa-
normus, (the port of the ancient Branchidæ, in

the district of Miletus) now called *Iéronda*. It
was the object of the Capitan Pasha to return
with the united fleet to Samos. On the 8th and
9th September the Turkish vessels attempted in
vain to effect a passage through the channel between Calymna and the coast of Caria, the wind
not being favourable, and the Greeks advancing
to meet them. On the 10th they were still more
unfortunate. Early in the morning they had advanced with a favourable breeze against the enemy, who was becalmed near Calymna; and the
nearest of the Greek vessels, exposed to the
heavy fire of the Turkish ships, were in danger
of being destroyed, or at least of being cut off
from the rest of the fleet, when a breeze arising,
the Greek ships were enabled to act more in concert. Such a desultory combat, as the great inferiority of the Greek vessels will alone admit of,
was kept up until the middle of the day, when
two fireships were attached to a large Egyptian
brig of war, and not long afterwards two others
to the frigate which commanded the Tunisine
division. So confounded were the Turks with
the boldness and skill of their opponents in thus
attacking them with their small vessels, in the
open sea and under sail, that not even the Greek

ships accompanying the incendiary vessels suffered
much from the Turkish fire.   The Ottoman fleet
returned in confusion to the anchorage near
Budrúm (Halicarnassus), and the burning ships
drifting ashore, were entirely consumed.   Many
of the seamen were drowned or slain in endeavouring to escape from the flames, but the Tunisine commander was taken, and remains a
prisoner with the Greeks.

After this defeat the principal object of the
Capitan Pasha seems to have been that of effecting a safe retreat to the Dardanelles.   Some ships
of war having been left for the protection of the
transports which had been sent to the upper part
of the gulf of Cos to land the Egyptian troops,
the remainder, as soon as the calms, (which usually
prevail for some weeks after the cessation of the
Etesian winds) had given place to the equinoctial
gales, took advantage of a southerly breeze, and
after meeting with some interruption and loss near
Icaria, reached *Mytilíni*.

On the 7th October, the Turkish admiral,
having left Ibrahim Pasha in the command of the
naval forces, re-entered the Dardanelles.   About
the middle of the same month, Ibrahim, after
some unsuccessful encounters with the Greeks

near Chios and *Mytilíni*, returned to the Egyptian
armament in the gulf of Cos, and in the month of
November his ships sustained considerable damage
from the enemy on the northern coast of *Candia*.

If neither the Ottoman army in Thessaly can
succour the fortresses at the entrance of the gulf
of Corinth by land nor their navy by sea, as appears highly probable, those garrisons must be
left to their own resources.   We learn that Patræ
is now invested with a large body of land forces,
and that such a number of Greek vessels is stationed at the entrance of the gulf as has justified
the government of the Ionian islands in issuing a
proclamation enjoining all vessels bearing the insular flag to respect the blockade of the gulf.
This proclamation was dated from Corfú, on the
17th November.

At no period of the contest have the prospects
of the insurgents received such a rapid improvement as in the last six months.   In the beginning
of June, the persons forming the civil government
were engaged in open hostility with their own
military chieftains, who had shut them out from
their capital and principal fortress of Nauplia.
They had to prepare for the campaign with exhausted means; they had not yet received any

part of the loan which had been raised in London
by their agents four months before; and they
were in daily expectation of an attack from an
armament composed of the combined forces of all
the Musulman powers of the Mediterranean, the
most formidable that had yet been collected
against them.

It was under these desperate circumstances,
that the executive, alarmed at their danger, and
indignant at seeing among the transports hired at
Constantinople and Alexandria, a great number
of European flags, issued on the 8th June from
the Mills of Nauplia, (the ancient Lerne,) an edict,
authorising their cruizers to attack, burn, and
sink, with their ships' companies, all the European
vessels which they should find so employed.

We know by the experience of our own history,
how difficult a question of international law is that
of the extent of a belligerent's right to search,
detain, or capture a neutral vessel; and the question is certainly not simplified by the circumstances
of the present contest. No wonder then that
men so unread and unpractised as the persons
administering the government of Greece should
have fallen into an error on this occasion. The
tenor and tendency of the Greek orders, however,

had they been ever so right in principle, were too piratical to pass unnoticed. It was necessary to obviate the danger to which Maltese or other vessels under the British flag or protection might be exposed from the cruelty or thirst of plunder of any uncommissioned ruffian, who might take advantage of the Greek decree.

It seems to have been very reluctantly that the British government proceeded to adopt strong measures on this occasion, for it was not until the 6th of September, three months after the date of the Greek manifesto, that a proclamation was issued at *Corfú*, notifying that, in consequence of the refusal of the Greek government to annul the obnoxious decree, our admiral in the Mediterranean had been directed to seize and detain all armed vessels acknowledging the authority of the provisional government of Greece.

The Greek edict was rescinded by a new proclamation from Nauplia, according to which the Greek seamen were instructed that merchant ships under European flags, carrying stores and provisions without troops, had the privileges of neutrality, and were to be subject only to the usages existing under the same circumstances among European powers: which usages, it is to be supposed, cannot protect them from the fortune of war, from capture, and even destruction, in case of their being found in company with and aiding a military operation of the enemy.

This new decree of the Greek government was speedily followed by another, requiring all Greek privateers to furnish themselves with commissions from the government; and thus amicably terminated the most serious of those inevitable collisions that has yet occurred between the delegated authorities of the Greek insurrection and the government of the western islands of Greece. The event will have been a lesson doubly useful to the Greeks, should it lead to the conviction that they are fortunate in having a neighbour who, from political necessity, is a vigilant observer of their conduct; who is qualified, by superior knowledge and experience, to give them the advice best calculated to keep them in the road of their true interests; and whose inclinations prompt him to bestow upon them all the assistance, compatible with the neutrality which is essential to the maintenance of the general peace of Europe.

LONDON, *January*, 1825.

THE close of 1824 arrived without the accomplishment of any of the great designs announced by the Porte in the beginning of that year. Of the forces enumerated in the plan of campaign which has been mentioned, the Egyptians had proceeded no farther than Crete, while the armies ordered for Northern Greece had either not been assembled at all or had dwindled into small bodies which had performed nothing of importance. By the experience of the three preceding summers there remained no hope to the Porte of making an impression upon the Moréa from the northward, without the simultaneous debarkation of a large and well appointed force on some part of the Peloponnesian coast; but the finances as well as the military ardour of the provinces of Europe and Asia were too much exhausted to render that easy in 1825 which had so thoroughly failed in 1822. As long, however, as any of the fortresses of the Moréa remained in possession of the Turks there was some prospect of success, and as the Pasha of Egypt entered cordially into the war, prompted apparently by a Musulman feeling, by the importance to him at all times of a good

understanding with the Porte, by the flourishing
state of his treasury, and by the hope of at least
of retaining to himself Crete and Cyprus ; the
Ottoman government was by his means furnished
with an army for debarkation, to the providing of
which their own resources were insufficient. They
continued deaf, therefore, to any suggestions for
entering into a compromise with the insurgents,
they flattered themselves that the effort of 1825
would be decisive, and the assurance was carefully
repeated in every part of Europe by the enemies
of Greek independence.

It may be supposed that it was not without
some hesitation that the Porte resolved upon thus
tacitly giving up both *Candia* and the *Moréa* to the
already too powerful Mehmet Aly ; but it was the
least of two evils ; the chief pecuniary burthen of
the war would be thrown upon him, the rest they
left to Kismét or destiny—to those chances from
treachery or accident, which have seldom allowed
a troublesome provincial governor to die a natural
death, and still less frequently to bequeath his
authority to his family.

To those politicians who endeavour to persuade
the Greeks that their views of independence are
premature, it must be admitted that the insurrec-

tion has been so in one respect. It never before
happened that Egypt had a Turkish Viceroy of
such talent, ambition and good-fortune as to effect
military conquest beyond the limits of his government, at the same time that he filled foreign harbours with his merchandize,—and who, though,
like a true Turk, he has no other object than personal gratification through the misery of the
great body of his subjects, is certainly a formidable power at the present moment.

By turning into his own coffers the greatest
part of the land-revenue and of the commercial
profits of Egypt, by improving the inexhaustible
agricultural resources of that country, and particularly by his good fortune in raising a species
of cotton, eagerly purchased for the manufactures of England,* he has created a revenue very
far exceeding that of any of his predecessors,
while his ambition has prompted him to expend
those treasures in the increase of his military
establishment, which now amounts to forty thou-

* Upwards of a million sterling is stated to have been paid
for Egyptian cotton imported into England in one year ; of
this the Pasha monopolizes both the purchase from the grower,
and the sale to the merchant. Thus it appears, that both the
contending parties in Greece are now supporting the war
with finances derived from England.

M

sand men, with a fleet of thirty vessels of war. That which the Greeks have been prevented from attaining, by disunion, by a want of government and by the constant pressure of immediate danger,—Mehmet Aly, having to consult only his single will, has in a very short time accomplished, namely, the formation of a body of infantry, instructed in the European use of the musket, and which, although their discipline is probably as yet imperfect, have at least acquired an advantage of great importance against the irregular troops of an anarchical people, that of obedience and the habit of acting as a single body.

Who could have foreseen even a year ago, that the Pasha of Egypt should so suddenly have increased his financial resources: or that his wealth should have attracted to his military service a great number of unemployed officers from France and other parts of Europe:* or that he should

---

* The influx of French officers into Egypt may lead to important consequences, unless Mehmet Aly should take the alarm, before the Europeans have made such a progress in organizing an army similar to that of the native troops of British India, as could not fail to give them great power and influence in the country. It is not intended to infer that the French government has any ambitious designs in encouraging

so quickly have mastered a difficulty which has
hitherto been found insurmountable by any Turkish government, namely, that of bringing his army
to submit to European discipline : or that he
should so heartily have entered at an immense expense into designs, which with the most favourable
result are more calculated to gratify a dangerous
ambition than to serve his real interests.   The
event has totally changed the nature of the war
in Greece, which before, although slowly, seemed
to be surely leading to an independence *de facto*,
which would have been the best preliminary to a
pacification.*

this emigration ; perhaps it has no other view at present than
that of finding employment for a large portion of the needy
survivors of the army of Bonaparte.   But it is not difficult to
conceive that circumstances may arise out of the proceeding,
well calculated to suggest such designs.   The *strictest virtue*
cannot always resist temptation, and nations have been known
by a dexterous management in peace, to regain what has been
lost on the field of battle.

  * In the same manner as Spanish American independence
has been established without even the apprehension of any war
with the power that lately ruled those countries.   The Turks
are a people seldom diverted from their purposes but by fear,
and to move them the danger must be imminent; but it is
equally in their character to submit when they are conscious
that what is actually done cannot be reversed by any exertions
of theirs, though it might be a most arduous task to obtain their
previous concurrence in the same measure.   Unhappily the

Unhappily for the Greek cause, the numerical strength of the Turks in Crete had, by the assistance of the Egyptians, produced a temporary suppression of the insurrection in that important island, which thus furnished Ibrahim Pasha, the son and lieutenant of Mehmet Aly, with great facilities of communication between Egypt and the Moréa, and thus enabled him to begin the campaign of 1825, without waiting for the return of spring.

In the middle of February, Ibrahim made a landing at *Mothóni* and *Koróni ;* a second debarkation followed in the beginning of March, and before the end of that month, a battery had been erected against the small fortified town of *Neó-Kastro,* or *New Navarin.* This place, which had been taken by the Greeks in the first year of

present state of the war in Greece leaves but a distant prospect of pacifying the country in the manner alluded to; and there seems no other mode than that which is recommended by an eloquent writer who was not long since minister for foreign affairs in France. " Qu'on dise simplement à la cour Ottomane, (dans une depêche collective, ou des depêches simultanées addressées par les puissancés chretiennes au Divan,) Reconnoissez l'indépendance de la Grèce ou avec des conditions ou sans conditions; si vous ne voulez pas prendre ce parti, nous serons forcés nous-mêmes de reconnoître cette indépendance pour le bien de l'humanité en général, pour la paix de l'Europe en particulier, pour les intérêts du commerce."— *Chateaubriand, Note sur la Grèce.*

the war, instead of having been repaired and strengthened, instead of having conduced in their hands to the security of the harbour, one of the most important in Greece by its capacity, commodiousness and position ; instead of having led to the acquisition of *Mothóni* and *Koróni*, and to the safety of all the southern part of the Peninsula, had been left nearly in the same state in which it was taken from the Turks in 1821, consisting of a low wall without any ditch, flanked on the land-side by some small bastions, and still weaker towards the sea, where it had received only a slight patching, since it was battered by the Russians, from one of the opposite islands, in the year 1770.

The larger of these two islands, the celebrated scene of one of the few triumphs of Athens over Sparta, and destined once more to deserve the name of Sphacteria, is two miles in length, and a quarter of a mile broad. It covers a noble basin of six miles in circumference, which has an entrance of six hundred yards between *Neó-Kastro* and the south eastern end of Sphacteria ; the northern end of the same island being separated, by a channel of one hundred yards, from a peninsular promontory anciently called Coryphasium.

A ruined castle* of the middle ages, which
stands upon the summit of this Cape, on the site
of the ancient Pylus, was occupied by the Greeks ;
the hill is steep and rocky, and a large lagune on
the land-side, separated from the sea at either
end of the promontory by a narrow strip of land,
renders the position naturally very strong. But
the castle having neither been repaired nor armed,
was incapable of defence against a very superior
force ; and being commanded, at the distance of
one thousand yards, by the highest point of
Sphacteria, there remained little hope to the
Greeks of preserving either of their posts at
Navarin, unless they could retain possession of
the island by the assistance of their ships, eight
or ten of which were anchored in the harbour.

The army of Ibrahim Pasha consisted of about
ten thousand infantry, two thousand Albanians,
and an adequate proportion of cavalry and artillery.
After several desultory actions with small bodies
of Armatolí, he attacked on the 19th of April,
and completely defeated in their position, threat-
ening the road from *Neó-Kastro* to *Mothóni,* all
the troops which the President Kundurioti had

* The modern Greek name of this castle is 'Αβαρῖνος,—
whence the Italian names of *Old* and *New Navarin.*

been able to collect, amounting to about six thousand men. To take Sphacteria was the next
object of Ibrahim, but it was not until the arrival
of his ships from *Suda* in *Candia,* with a third
division of land forces, that he found it convenient to put this design into execution.

On the 8th of May a landing was made from
the fleet, at the same time that Ibrahim made a
show of attacking *Old Navarin.* Sphacteria had
been occupied by four or five hundred Greeks
detached from the two fortresses, the remaining
garrisons of which did not amount to more than
two thousand men. At the moment of assault, all
the Greek vessels, except one whose commander
was in the island, made their escape out of the harbour, in order to join the squadron of Miaoulis,
which had followed the Turkish fleet and was in
sight in the offing. Receiving no farther assistance
either from the fortresses or the Greek ships, the
unfortunate defenders of the island were left to
be cut to pieces by the very superior numbers
who landed from the Turkish fleet. Mavrokor-
dato and the commandant of *Neó-Kastro,* both of
whom happened to be in the island, had the good
fortune to save themselves on board the remaining ship, which fought its way with great gallantry

through the Turkish fleet; but its commander
Psamado, one of the most distinguished Ydriote
seamen, Count Santa Rosa, whose name is well
known in the Piedmontese attempt at revolution,
in 1820, and several Greeks who have acted a
prominent part in the insurrection, fell in the
island, together with the greater part of the
troops. Two days afterwards the Greeks in *Old
Navarin* capitulated on condition of laying down
their arms and retiring; and the Turkish ships
having entered the harbour, opened a fire upon
Neó-Kastro. About fifty pieces of cannon were
placed in battery on the land-side, but it was
not until the 23d of May that, after a week
consumed in negociation, the garrison marched
out on the same terms as those of *Avaríno*, and
were embarked in European vessels for *Kalamáta*.
By the affair of the 8th they had been deprived
of their commander, they had lost by the same
disaster the provisions and stores which had not
yet been landed from the Greek ships, and the
aqueduct which supplied the place with water had
been at an early period cut off by the Turks,—
so that the transactions at Navarin, although not
much calculated to adorn the Greek annals, serve
at least to show that their disunion and unskilful-

ness are fully compensated by an equal want of skill and a greater want of activity on the part of the enemy. The Greeks had not suffered so severely on any occasion since the beginning of the war; more than two hundred fell in the actions near New Navarin, and a much greater number in the island, together with near one hundred of their invaluable seamen.

Ibrahim soon afterwards sustained a naval loss at *Mothóni*, which, although highly honourable to Greek enterprize, was not of sufficient magnitude materially to affect the operations of the Ottoman fleet. After the capture of Sphacteria, six ships of war and about thirty transports were followed by Miaoulis into the harbour of *Mothóni*, where more than half of them were destroyed by the Greek fire-ships.

When *Neó-Kastro* capitulated, the Moréa had already been abandoned by the Greek troops of Northern Greece, and was left to the defence of its native Armatolí. It was particularly upon the former brave men that the loss on the 19th April had fallen, and as they had heard of the arrival of Reshid Pasha as Seraskier in Epirus, and of his approach with a large force to *Mesolonghi*, it would have been impossible, under these

circumstances, for the Œtæan and Ætolian chiefs
to keep their followers from proceeding to the
defence of their own mountains, had they been
ever so well inclined. These troops, it is to be
observed, had entered the peninsula in the preceding autumn by the orders or rather at the persuasion of the government, which by their means
had frustrated an attempt of Kolokotroni, in union
with some of the leading primates of the Moréa,
to change the executive power by force of arms.
In consequence of the event of this conspiracy,
Kolokotroni, at the time of the retreat of the
Northern Armatolí from the Moréa, was a prisoner in Ydra; but, abandoned by the troops of
Northern Greece, the executive body had no
other resource than that of restoring the military
power into the hands in which alone the Moreite
troops had confidence. An amnesty was therefore published, and Kolokotroni, protesting all ob-
livion of the past, proceeded to collect the Armatolí of the peninsula, in order to oppose the advance of the Egyptians.

In the beginning of June a detachment of Ibrahim's army defeated a body of Greeks at *Aghiá*,
on the mountain which overhangs the town of
Arkadhiá (the ancient Cyparissus); and about the

same time the Pasha himself occupied *Kalamáta*,
at the opposite extremity of Messenia, thus becoming master of all the resources of this fertile
portion of the peninsula. From *Kalamáta* he
soon began his march into the interior. After
having sustained some loss from the troops of
Kolokotróni in crossing the mountain now called
Makriplághi, which separates the plain of Mes-
sene from the valley of Megalopolis or the Upper
Alpheius, he occupied, on the 20th June, the
abandoned and half-demolished Tripolitza, and
hastening to profit by his advantages, appeared
before Nauplia in one month after the capture of
Neó-Kastro. A division of his army attacked the
Greek outposts at the Mills of Nauplia on the 25th
June, but without success; although the Greeks
under Demetrius Ypsilanti (who had been living
for the last two or three years retired from affairs
at Tripolitza) had, in no part of the action, more
than a few hundred men, supported by the fire
of some small armed vessels anchored near the
shore.

Having failed in his principal design, that of
surprising Nauplia or of intimidating it into terms
of capitulation, Ibrahim retreated from the Argolis, and endeavoured to attain the next most im-

portant object, that of opening a passage to *Patra;*
but the mountainous districts of Arcadia and
Achaia, which are interposed between that city
and the plains of Mantineia and Argos, are exactly suited to such troops as the Armatolí of
Greece; and though these were unable, as well
from their numbers as their want of discipline, to
face the Egyptians in a general action, or to in-
terrupt the Pasha's communications with the
Messenian ports, Ibrahim, on his part, has suffered considerable loss from sickness as well as
from the sword, and has only been able to over-
run the plains and to reduce all the most fertile
parts of the country to that desolation which pro-
verbially attends the footsteps of a Turkish sol-
dier, even in peace. And thus was annihilated in
a few weeks that slight improvement which had
been produced by a three years' exemption from
the blighting presence of the Musulmans, during
which an increase of inhabitants seeking refuge
from other parts of Greece, together with the confidence inspired by a government which, however
imperfect, had been sufficiently composed of right
materials to produce some beneficial reforms,
promised in a short time to effect a favourable
change in the whole peninsula. Schools of mutual

instruction and other places of education had been established in several towns, and no sooner had the government obtained the power of taking the collection of the revenue out of the hands of the old primates and captains of Armatolí, than the national domains formed of the confiscated Turkish property were let for double the sum that had been given for them in the preceding year.

In Northern Greece the war has been a repetition of that of the former campaigns with little variation. The same military plan (and in fact no other can well be devised) has produced similar movements, while the same defects in the Turkish system, without any abatement in the rude activity and courage which characterizes the Greeks, has led to similar failures.

About the same time that the Egyptian army occupied Messenia, the Osmanlys moved from Epirus and Thessaly upon the shores of the Corinthiac gulf: a Turkish division, making a rapid movement from *Zitúni,* seized upon *Sálona,* and in the end of April the Seraskier Reshid Pasha appeared before *Mesolónghi.* But he came quite unprovided with heavy artillery; the Ottoman fortresses at the entrance of the gulf were unable to supply him to any great extent, and the

Greeks were successful in interrupting his communications with *Salona* and with Thessaly, through the mountains of Locris and Ætolia. Contracting his plan, therefore, the Seraskier recalled into Thessaly the troops which had entered Bœotia for the purpose of supporting the operations of the Pasha of *Egripo*, and reinforcing himself from Larissa, he directed all his means to the blockade of *Mesolonghi*, and to the protection of his position before that place, from the dangers with which it was continually threatened from the Ætolian mountains. The experience as well of the present as of the preceding year had shown him that no dependence could be placed on any of the Albanians, except the Gheghe or Roman Catholics of the province of Scodra, and he looked forward with anxiety to the arrival of the fleet of the Capitan Pasha, which was to bring him materials for the siege, to furnish boats for attacking the place on the side of the lagune, and to secure his communication with Patra from the interruption to which it was liable whenever the Greek cruizers made their appearance.

The Turkish admiral sailed from the Dardanelles in the end of May; about the first of June

he was met in the channel of *Cavo Doro* (Capharea), by the Ydriote Sakhturi, who destroyed
with his fire-ships three Turkish men of war and
several transports; another corvette was run
ashore by the crew and burnt in the island of
Syra. These vessels contained a large proportion of the stores intended for the siege of Mesolonghi. A few days afterwards the Capitan Pasha
entered *Suda*, where he joined the Egyptian fleet
lately returned from *Navarino*. He was quickly
followed by the joint forces of Miaouli and Sakhturi, amounting to about 70 sail. On the 14th,
two days after their arrival, they attacked a division of the Ottoman fleet which remained in the
outer harbour of Suda, and at the expense of
three fire-ships, destroyed a corvette with its
equipage. They were prevented from any further success, not so much by the strength or
vigilant fears of the enemy, as by the narrow-
ness of the entrance into the inner bay of Suda,
and by the fortified island which protects it.

A few days afterwards the Greek fleet was dispersed by a tempest, when finding themselves deprived of their means of offence, by a deficiency
of fire-ships, they retired to Ydra, leaving the
Turkish admiral to proceed unmolested to Na-

varin, where he landed a reinforcement of 5000
men. From thence he pursued his course with
seven frigates and many smaller vessels to Mesolonghi, where he arrived about the 10th July.
The Turkish garrisons at the entrance of the gulf
of Corinth then received the supplies of which
they stood in need; the Seraskier pressed the
siege of Mesolonghi with increased vigour, the
boats of the Ottoman fleet entered the lagunes,
and on the first of August the Turkish commanders, apprehensive of the approach of the
Greek fleet, ordered a general attack. The
works on the land side were assailed in four
places, while thirty boats occupied the lake. The
Osmanlys, however, were every where repulsed;
and the Greek fleet, consisting of about 25
brigs, having quickly made its appearance, succeeded in destroying two small ships of war,
as well as all the boats on the lagune,—in relieving Mesolonghi,—and in forcing the Turkish
fleet to retreat, a part of it retiring behind the
castles of the gulf of Corinth, while others made
sail for the Ægæan, whither they were speedily
followed by a detachment of the Greek vessels.

The Armatolí at the same time attacked the
Ottoman camp and opened a momentary commu-

nication with the Greek garrison, but the Seraskier has been sufficiently strong to maintain his position without much interruption, and as late as the end of October he continued to besiege Mesolonghi, though with scarcely any result except that of loss to his own troops. It seems probable that the garrison, open as it is to relief by sea, will be able to sustain all such attempts until a great part of the Ottoman forces will assuredly on the approach of winter retire from their desolate and exposed situation, whether such a movement may be agreeable to their commander or not.

The Porte however appears to entertain hopes of pursuing operations through the winter. The Capitan Pasha from the Ægæan proceeded to Alexandria, where, in the middle of October, thirty ships of war with a fleet of transports, containing (it is said) eight thousand Egyptians, were ready to sail for the Moréa; it would seem therefore that the perseverance with which, according to the latest accounts, the Seraskier retained his position before *Mesolonghi*, had in view the assistance which he expected speedily to derive from this new Egyptian expedition.

It cannot be doubted that the unfortunate loss of *Navarin* has given the Turks a vast addition

N

of means for prosecuting naval operations on the western coast of Greece, and particularly in relation to the important positions at the entrance of the gulf of Corinth; but the present season is favourable to the garrison of Mesolonghi as well by sea as by land, and if the Greeks have only as much obstinacy as their enemies, that place ought not to capitulate until the Egyptians have effected the conquest of the northern part of the Moréa, or until the promiscuous rabble that man the Turkish ships have learnt to retain possession of the road of Mesolonghi in face of the Greek seamen. How far either of these suppositions may be realized in the ensuing year we shall not pretend to foresee.

Upon reviewing the events of the contest since its first commencement in the summer of 1821, it will be seen how little has been done on either side, in a military point of view, towards its decisive termination; such children are both parties in the art of war, and so contemptible will their operations both by land and water generally appear to the military critics of civilized Europe. But there are two advantages possessed by the Greeks which ought to prevent them from despairing of final success—the strength of their country and the superiority of their seamen. The skill, the activity, and often the gallantry of the Greek sailors, have excited the approbation of some of our own sea-officers. It is true that neither the numbers nor size of their vessels are such as can give them the command of the sea, or ensure to them such a protracted blockade of the maritime fortresses as will lead to a surrender caused by famine, or prevent debarkations, such as those which have occurred during the present year, especially as long as the Greeks are unable to undertake a regular siege of the maritime fortresses. But the Turkish seamen always avoid the Greeks, and the Turkish squadrons are almost sure of receiving some damage whenever they meet. Their *brulotiers* in particular have furnished examples of enterprise and patriotic devotion, which are fully sufficient to establish the national character, and to cancel the disgrace of any conduct that may have occurred of an opposite kind, the unavoidable consequence of insubordination and of a privation of law both civil and military.*

* The skill and enterprise of the Greek seamen has not met with its merited success this summer. Had the bold attempt made in the month of August to burn the Ottoman armament in the port of Alexandria been successful, it would have greatly altered the present aspect of affairs.

In the strength of their mountainous districts the Greeks have a still firmer anchor for their hopes. The more exposed parts of Greece, such as Crete, Macedonia, and Eastern Thessaly, may enter into temporary terms with the enemy, but this cannot occur in that great citadel of mountains which extends from the plains of Thessaly and Bœotia, westward as far as the sea-coast, and southward as far as the centre of the Moréa—at least until the Ottomans are much farther advanced in conquest than they are at present. It might be supposed that military ignorance being nearly equal on both sides, the party which should first establish a disciplined force, and which should first obtain any important assistance from European officers of military experience, would be almost certain of success. But the discipline of the Egyptian infantry is not as yet, we apprehend, of a very high degree, and there is wanting in the Egyptian army the education, the intelligence, and those martial habits in every gradation of officers, without which the proficiency of the troops in the European use of the musket must lose a great part of its advantage. Mehmet Aly is yet far from having overcome those numerous vices in the Turkish

system, both civil and military, which so often render Turkish councils abortive. The desolation
of the Moréa, together with the inefficacy of a
Turkish commissariat, will place perpetual obstacles in the way of Ibrahim's progress, and will
render the arduous task of subduing the mountains of Greece still more difficult. That tracta-
bility of disposition which has enabled Mehmet
Aly to mould his Egyptians to the European discipline, is allied to an inferiority in hardihood and
energy to the European and Asiatic Turks, with
whom similar attempts have always failed. The
Egyptians are precisely the troops least adapted
to face the active and hardy Greek in the rude
climate, the barren soil, and the strong positions
of his native mountains. We cannot easily conceive that Greece is destined to be subjugated by
Egyptians. Even Sesostris drove his conquering
chariot no farther than Thrace: nor will those who
have had an opportunity of comparing the Greek
with the Egyptian of the present day, think it
probable that a conquest will now be effected, if
it depends upon the military qualities of the
two people. In short, as not even Spain in the
time of the Romans was better adapted for pro-
longing an obstinate contest, by the strength of

the country and the elastic character of the inhabitants,* there is the fairest reason to hope that Mehmet Aly may be tired of his present expensive undertaking before he has made any great progress towards its completion—a result which is rendered still more probable if it be true that his commercial speculations with England are likely to be much less profitable in the present than they have been in the preceding year. If, with all the exertions of the Pasha of Egypt the Porte should now fail in becoming masters of the two great bulwarks of the insurrection—Mesolonghi and Nauplia, it may be said that they have put forth their utmost exertions in vain and that their future hopes will rest upon the effects of perseverance and of the superiority of their foreign assistance.

In addition to the two principal advantages which have been mentioned, the cause of the Greeks derives considerable strength and hope from the impossibility on their part of submitting to such a state of vassalage as they were before subject to. They know too well, that to give the Turks

* Hispania non quam Italia modo sed quam ulla pars terrarum bello reparando aptior erat, locorum hominumque ingeniis. *Liv.* l. xxviii. c. xii.

such a power would be to consent to their own destruction: and they did not want the declaration of Ibrahim to be assured that if he should acquire the government of the Moréa by right of conquest, which the Porte has promised him, he would exchange the enslaved survivors of the peninsula for a colony of Egyptians. Such a termination, however, all history as well as common reason tell us is impossible if the Greeks have but " the unconquerable will and courage never to submit and yield." The utmost that can be expected is the retreat of a great part of the population of Greece into the mountains, a continuance of predatory warfare on both sides, and the desolation of every other part of the country, except perhaps the immediate vicinity of the fortified places. Some politicians will perhaps be inclined to say that, however deplorable to the people of Greece such a result might be, it would be better that they should suffer than that the general peace of Europe should be compromised. But supposing the interior continent of Greece to be thus comfortably settled for the general repose, there still remains an extensive sea-coast—in fact the numerous islands, the winding shores, and the great proportion of maritime outline to the size of

the country, render the Greeks more peculiarly a
naval people than any other in Europe.   If forced
to the extremity of distress they must be pirates
by sea as well as freebooters by land.   However
disposed the nation might be to a better course,
however deserving of a better fate, necessity
would force the maritime population to those
habits of life, which are natural to Greece in a
savage state, and to which its rocky creeks and
islands have always afforded and will ever give
the greatest facilities.   No alternative would then
remain for the powers of Europe, but to give up
all commercial pursuits in the Levant or to suppress the Greek piracies by force—in other words,
to assist the Turks in exterminating them from
their native islands.

It cannot be doubted that the Porte with its pro-
verbially slow and persevering policy looks forward
to this ultimate result; to the gradual effects of
distress in rendering the insurgents utterly lawless,
until with loss of character they shall lose the sympathy which is now excited in their favour, and
shall not have a partizan in Europe sturdy enough
to espouse their cause.   They may then, it is
hoped, by the agency of menace, fraud or bri-
bery upon leading individuals or separate com-

munities, be induced in detail to offer submission
and to accept the amnesty of the Porte. Similar
views seem to be entertained by those *civilized*
opponents of the emancipation of Greece in the
courts of Europe, who have imitated the Porte in
incessantly predicting the complete defeat of the
insurgents in *another* campaign.

On the other hand the longer this contest lasts,
the more incredible it becomes, that Christian
Europe will contemplate unmoved the destruction
of a Christian people by the semi-barbarous followers of a religion hostile to the whole Christian
name, because those infidels have for some centuries been suffered to abuse the possession of
some of the finest countries in Europe, and because, in consideration of their proximity and for
the sake of the general peace, they have in some
degree been admitted into the social system of
the civilized world. In a case of extremity it is
difficult to conceive any other result than that the
great powers should agree in procuring a pacification, or that their disagreement upon the subject
should lead to a war.

It is reported that one of these powers is desirous
of seeing the Greeks reduced as nearly as possible
to their former state of vassalage; that another

wishes the whole country to be formed into three principalities after the fashion of Moldavia and Wallachia; while it seems to be the desire of the nations which do not border on the Turkish empire, and which come into contact with the Greeks only by sea, that some part at least of the country should form an independent state. To Great Britain in particular such a consummation is particularly desirable. The principal reasons are too obvious to require mentioning: it is sufficient to allude to the nautical and commercial character of the Greek people, to the necessity of maintaining our high station in the Mediterranean against powerful rivals more conveniently situated, and whom to suspect of having designs both upon Greece and Egypt will always be a salutary presumption—to the positions which, with a prospective policy of this kind, we have now for fifteen years held in Greece itself.

In attempting to devise an arrangement for the pacification of Greece, the following considerations, some of which have already been adverted to in a preceding part of this·memoir, seem to be the most important.

1. That in every part of the Turkish empire, but especially in Europe and in the maritime parts

of Asia, the superior intelligence and industry of
the Greeks have rendered the Turks greatly dependent upon them in the transaction of affairs,
political as well as commercial and domestic, and
that hence arises a permanent bond of connexion
between the two people on the basis of reciprocal
advantage which would promote tranquillity, if the
Greeks had that security against Turkish extortion and religious intolerance which can only be
completely afforded by a place of refuge among
their own countrymen.

2. That the chief obstacles (independently of
the existing war) to the internal tranquillization
of Greece and to the formation of a stable government is the very uncivilized nature of its
military population added to the contiguity of
Albania, where a large portion of a still more uncivilized people is under the necessity of finding
employment as soldiers.

3. That an extensive land frontier to liberated
Greece would render much more sensible the influence of the soldiery both of Greece and Albania, at the same time that all the foreign relations
of an infant government would become more difficult and complicated.

4. That the agricultural and commercial capa-

bilities of the Moréa are so great, that it would
not be too densely peopled with ten times its
present population.

5. That a modified principle of actual possession appears to be the only basis of pacification
practicable under *existing circumstances:* in other
words, that however disposed European media-
tors may be to favour the Christian party, the
Turks cannot be required to give up much more
than they have lost, nor the Greeks be supported
in demanding much more than they have really
gained by the war—the chief object of any interference of the powers of Europe in this question, being the future security of this Christian
people from the cruel oppression under which
they have so long been suffering.

With these main considerations in view, the
following appears to be the most practicable plan
for the benefit of Greece at the present moment.

1. The Peloponnesus, together with all the European islands except Crete, to form an independent state under the system of government which
has already been in part established, but subject
to such improvements as experience may have
shewn desirable.

It has already been remarked that the physical

construction of the country, and the evidence of ancient history, as well as the national feeling and opinion, so strongly shewn by the meeting of deputies from various parts of Greece in the years 1822 and 1823, all equally tend to prove that a central representation of the islands and districts, with a municipal government to each of them, is the most natural constitution of government for Greece, and such we are persuaded it will always in great measure be, whatever may be the form of the central executive administration.

It has been strongly argued against rendering any part of Greece independent, that the people are as yet unfit for such a task—that they are at present incapable of governing themselves. But the same was long said of the Spanish American States, which we now find gradually settling into governments that may be treated with. If Greece emerges from an infinitely more degrading servitude than that of Spanish America, there are many Greeks on the other hand who have profited by that advantage which their country possesses over America, in its vicinity to the most civilized part of the world—an advantage which would be attended with the most rapid effects, if Greece were restored to freedom.

Without denying that the Greeks inherit the contentious character of their ancestors, it may be argued in their favour that their failure in forming a government was the inevitable consequence of their previous condition and would have happened to any other people formed of similar elements. When it is considered that the military defence of the country by land has, from the beginning of the insurrection, been in the hands of an irregular soldiery, who, although they possess some great virtues and deserve highly of their country, are the most unenlightened class in the nation, and that the leaders of this militia are in general persuaded that their interests are opposed to the formation of a civil government, it is not surprising that such circumstances, added to the constant imminence of external danger, should have paralyzed all the efforts of men who for the most part were uneducated, who had been excluded from intercourse with enlightened society, and who were totally unpractised in the management of great affairs. We cannot be surprised that discord, which misfortune seldom fails to generate, should have arisen amongst these men themselves, or that whenever the difficulties which assailed them drove the better class from power, its seat should

have been occupied by selfishness, avarice and in-
capacity.   Such a cruel war as the Greeks have
been exposed to, has unsettled many a government
that had been established for ages ; no wonder
then, that it has prevented the formation of a
system of order where none previously existed.
So far from thinking that Greece possesses no men
adapted to the conduct of affairs, we believe that
there is scarcely any people among whom the natural
qualifications for such stations are more common,
though it will probably require some years of peace
and freedom to produce their complete develop-
ment.   Every failure of the Greeks in government
may be considered a lesson for the future and an
approximation to a better management; for that
such is the natural progress of society, Spanish
America, among many other examples, has shewn
and still continues to prove to us.   If, upon further
trial, the Greeks should still be found too unenlightened and contentious to establish order—if no
man should arise among them capable of supporting the central Executive authority, (for this
seems to be the great deficiency,) they may themselves see the necessity of resorting to foreign
assistance.

2. With respect to Greece beyond the Isthmus,

the difficulty of attaining tranquillity under a
mixed government of Greeks and Turks is, perhaps, not so great as at first sight may appear.
In fact, there has existed a system of this kind in
many parts of Greece ever since the Turkish
conquest. The Greeks never having been completely subdued, it has followed, that in those
parts of the country where the Turks could not
indulge their savage disposition without danger,
a compromise of power has generally been the
practical result.   In the parts of Greece most
exposed to Turkish oppression, no such middle
state could exist; but wherever it met with a
check, either from the strength of the country,
from the especial protection given by the Porte
to a favoured district, or from some more temporary and accidental cause,—where the fear of the
Turkish power was sufficiently strong at the same
time to repress the jealous character of the Greeks,
they have enjoyed a considerable share of order
and tranquillity under a municipal administration.
It was especially in those places where some pros-
perous branch of trade or art afforded a lucrative
employment to the Greek community, at the same
time that the situation of the place gave them
security, that these little republics were most

orderly: a βουλὴ of elders, precisely in the manner of the ancient Greek states, formed the governing power, which was supported by a stipendiary guard of Albanians or Armatolí. There were several flourishing communities of this description both in Northern Greece and the Moréa, the destruction or decline of which is to be dated, in the former division of the country to the increase of Aly Pasha's power, in the latter to the unfortunate expedition undertaken by Russia in the year 1770, which exposed the Peninsula to the alternate plunder of the Osmanlys and Albanians, and greatly reduced its population. The islands of the Ægæan Sea in like manner, though occasionally exposed to cruelty and insult from the Turkish fleet, or from pirates, were tolerably tranquil under Greek municipalities: and thus also, *Parga*, *Prévyza*, and *Vónitza*, for some years after the treaty of 1800, were happily administered under Venetian laws with an Aga residing on the part of the Porte.

If such a mode of government were established by the mediation of some of the European powers, and if the security of the Greeks were placed under their guarantee and the protection of their agents, it would probably not be long before

o

Greece, exclusively of the Moréa and the European islands, would be enabled, without any difficulty, to supply a revenue to the Sultan greater than he formerly derived from the whole country. The Albanian and Greek soldiers, being employed in considerable numbers, and regularly paid by the provincial or local governments, would thus be prevented from troubling the public tranquillity, while the Greek population, attending in security to agriculture, commerce, and education, would be following the surest road to a further improvement in their political condition.

Northern Greece might be divided into three governments, of which the chief places would be *Arta*, Larissa, and *Egripo;* Eubœa, according to this mode of pacification, being attached to the continent, and not considered one of the islands. Crete, Cyprus, Rhodes, Cos, Samos, Chios, Lesbos, Lemnos, might each constitute a separate government, tributary to the Porte, but secured from any interference of the Turks. In Crete, in the plains of Thessaly, and in the parts of Bœotia and Eubœa around *Egripo*, where Turkish individuals possess a considerable quantity of landed property, they might claim some share in the civil government; but the general effect of the new system would probably be, that many of them would dispose of their lands to the Greeks, and that they would gradually withdraw into Asia, or towards Constantinople.

In proposing the independence of the Moréa as the basis of the pacification of Greece, the writer does not wish to disguise, either from himself or his reader, that he has thought more of the interests of Greece and of Great Britain than of what may be agreeable to some of the other powers of Europe. At the same time he cannot avoid entertaining the opinion, that this is the only plan which promises to save the Turkish empire from destruction and Europe from a general war.

We have already observed that there are two other modes of disposing of this great question— to reduce Greece to its former condition, or to partition it into principalities under governors taken from the Greek families of Constantinople.

In reference to the former, it must be admitted that there is no tranquillity so profound as that of solitude and desolation—that it is by the operation of a principle somewhat similar that the Turkish empire has so long opposed a barrier to the conflicts of European avarice or ambition, on that fine field which is situated on the eastern side of the Mediterranean—and that it may be said, that if the Greeks chuse to submit their necks to the Turkish sabre, the nations of Christian Europe have no right to object to this mode of keeping the peace. But enough has been stated in the preceding pages to shew that such a result has now become scarcely possible. It may be a better mode of occupying the reader's time, therefore, to add a few words on the plan of forming Greece into principalities.*

It cannot be perceived that the advancement in knowledge, which has taken place among the Greeks during the last half century, has been, in

* The reader will find, in the *documents* appended to the Annual Register of 1825, a translation of the semi-official Russian paper which contains this latter plan, together with a remonstrance of M. Rodios, secretary of the Greek Executive, addressed to the British government, and Mr. Canning's reply. According to this plan, one principality was to consist of Eastern Greece, or of Thessaly, Bœotia and Attica; a second of Western Greece, or of Epirus, and Acarnania, from the Austrian boundary northward to the gulf of Corinth; the third of the Morea and Candia: the other islands to remain under a municipal government nearly in their former state. It may be thought, perhaps, that this plan differs little from that which we have suggested for Greece beyond the Isthmus; but the entire independence of a part of the country together with the latter, as an arrangement, rather intended to be provisional than permanent, makes a very wide difference in the two propositions.

any degree, the consequence of the connexion
with the Turkish subjects of the Greek church,
which Russia acquired in the years 1774, 1779,
and 1802; unless it be inasmuch as the Russian
flag was for some years very useful to the Greek
seamen in the islands; still less can that amelioration be attributed to the power which has been
delegated by the Porte to a small number of
Greeks during the last century. In short, there
seems little doubt that the formation of Greece
into governments, like those of the Ultra-Danubian provinces, would be almost as unfavourable
as its former state to that further moral improvement which must precede the complete admission
of the Greeks among the civilized people of
Europe. Is it that the proposers of this method
of pacifying the country are fearful of the example of Greek freedom upon their brethren of
the same church in the Russian dominions? is it
that hence they are desirous that the Greek character should not lose the defects which it has
acquired under the Turkish yoke, and that the
Greek, in every gradation of office, should still
closely resemble the Turk similarly situated?

But it is chiefly as tending to increase a power
already too formidable, as adding further strength

to the monarch who has declared the kingdom of
Poland and the grand duchy of Finland indisso-
lubly united to the Russian empire, as enabling
him to stretch his giant arms around Constantinople on the west, as he has already done towards
the frontiers of Persia on the east, that the plan
alluded to is most objectionable.

It has for many years been the general opinion,
that a hostile attack from Russia with all its
strength would be immediately fatal to the Turkish
empire in Europe.   The Porte, however, has
been sufficiently confident in the impediments to
such an undertaking, never to lower its tone towards the court of St. Petersburg to the degeee
which a contrary conviction would naturally have
produced, always trusting that such an attempt
would meet with great opposition from other
governments, and would probably give Turkey
several powerful allies.   The difficulties, in fact,
are not trifling.   As it would be impossible to
supply a large army in such an impoverished
country as Turkey, without the assistance of a
numerous fleet in the Black Sea, the preparation of which would require much time and
expense ;   and   as   every Turk is armed and
would be an obstinate defender of his own walls,

such a delay would be created, and such an immense Ottoman force would be collected around Constantinople, that a Russian army would be placed in the most imminent danger from Austria, in the rear, unless the operation had been previously combined with the latter power upon an understanding of mutual aggrandizement.

A gradual encroachment preparatory to ulterior conquest is the plan, therefore, that leads most surely to success. The relative position of Russia and Turkey would be very different from that which has prevailed for the last half century, if Greece had been previously for some time divided into principalities under Russian guarantee and inspection. Its governors and other persons in authority would then be little more than Russian agents, and during a preceding state of peace such a preparation might be made for a diversion to the southward, on any sudden assumption of hostilities, as would leave the Porte little chance of resistance on the northern side of the Bosphorus.

It would seem, therefore, that the Ottoman government should above all things be averse to the plan for governing Greece to which we have just alluded, and that it ought not to be indisposed to a friendly arrangement with the insurgents on the basis of a partial independence, by which measure alone it can hope in future to derive any useful assistance in war from the Greek seamen, whose loss it already severely feels. But the obstinacy of pride and ignorance, aided, perhaps, by the advice of some Europeans, trembling at the further dispansion of free principles, blinds the Porte to its real interests, and leads it to believe, that Greece may still be reduced to its former state of bondage.

LONDON, *December*, 1825.

NOTE

TO PAGE 5, LINE 13.

In adverting to the Histories or Memoirs of the Greek Insurrection which have been compiled in Europe, it is impossible to avoid some more particular notice of one of them, which, having been written by a person long resident in Greece, and who, while composing his work, was in correspondence with a brother remaining in that country, may be considered, from these circumstances, as entitled to the public confidence. The work to which we allude is the " Histoire de la Régénération de la Grèce," by M. Pouqueville. It consists of four volumes, in octavo, and includes the modern history of Greece, from the year 1740 to the end of 1823.

The author, as many of our readers may know, has already published two books of travels in Greece. The first, called " Voyage en Morée," appeared in the year 1805, in three volumes, octavo, and consisted of such very imperfect information as the author could collect during a close imprisonment at Tripolitza, and at Constantinople, added to that, which some of his comrades in captivity obtained under similar circumstances at Ioannina. The second work, intituled, " Voyage dans la Grèce," is in five thick and closely printed octavos, and contains the result of the author's observations during a residence of eleven years in Greece, in the capacity of consul-general of France.

One of the author's principal objects in these two

P

works (as it must be of all travellers in Greece) was an illustration of the ancient geographers and historians by means of topographical researches.   So well satisfied is he with the result of his labours, that he congratulates himself in the Preface to the " Voyage dans la Grèce," on having at length " débrouillé le cahos, qui couvrait l'antique Hellade." It appears, however, from M. Pouqueville's Narrative, that he travelled very little in any part of Northern Greece beyond the limits of Epirus; it is not surprising, therefore, that his attempts to describe districts which he never saw, and to accommodate mere oral information to the ancient authorities, have often produced erroneous results.   Even in Epirus, which he had such ample means of exploring during a ten years' residence at Ioannina, his conclusions are scarcely less defective than in the provinces which he had not personally examined.   Embarrassed where to place Dodona, he spreads the honours of the site over a space of twenty-five miles; he mistakes the ruins of Charadrus for those of Ambracia, and the river Arachthus for the Inachus, errors of such radical importance that they involve in absurdity the ancient geography of all the adjacent country.

In the Peloponnesus M. Pouqueville could not so easily go astray, that country being better known than Northern Greece; but having traversed only a few of the principal routes, he has added very little to the geographical information on the peninsula which the public already possessed.

The incorrectness with which M. Pouqueville writes the modern Greek names is by no means an unimportant defect in a work that aspires to be a guide to the geography of Greece. Sometimes he *Gallicizes* the names, as " Loroux, Dremichoux," for Λοῦρος, Τραμετζοῦς, " les monts Olichiniens," " les Haliacmonts," for the mountains called Ὀλύτζικα, Λιάκα, and often they are purposely distorted to support some favourite paradox, as in the instances of Iapouria, or Iapygia, Aidonia, Toxides, Caulonias, instead of Liaberí, Aidonát (the Turkish corruption of Saint Donatus), Toshke, Kolonia. which are the real modern names. The poverty of his acquisitions in Grecian geography is shown at once by the diminutive scale of his map, a single glance at which will equally prove its inaccuracy to every person acquainted with the country—Ioannina, the place of his long residence, instead of being nearly midway, as he places it, between the eastern and western coasts, is in truth only 32 geographical miles in direct distance from the nearest shore of Epirus, or between one third and one fourth part of the breadth of Northern Greece.

We have found it impossible to avoid these observations on M. Pouqueville's geography of Greece, because it has been necessary to enter briefly into the same subject in the present Memoir.

As to the " Histoire de la Régénération," we find it written in the same romantic and poetical style which prevails in the author's Travels, and which, although often very agreeably applied by him to local description and the representation of manners, is not so well suited to a statement of facts. Instead of a plain narrative, the author has entered into the supposed causes, combinations, and consequences of each trifling event; relating, as if he had been present, the speeches that were spoken, as well as the actions

p 2

that were performed, thus losing the confidence of
his reader by an attempt at precision, which it was
impossible for him, under the given circumstances, to
attain.   Nor is M. Pouqueville satisfied with displaying
his knowledge of each thought and movement of the
contending parties; he is equally competent to expose
the Machiavelic arts, as he is pleased to describe them,
of the agents of Great Britain; and he pretends to be
thoroughly instructed in every secret council of the
British Septinsular government, which he politely
entitles the Pandemonium of Corcyra.   In fact, it
appears to have been his main design, as a true disciple
of the Napoleon school, to throw blame and odium
upon England and Englishmen: but we may console
ourselves with the assurance that his authority will
neither be very extensive nor very durable.

ERRATUM.

Page 113, line 9, *for* "a mile broad,"
             read " two miles broad."

For EU product safety concerns, contact us at Calle de José Abascal, 56–1°,
28003 Madrid, Spain or eugpsr@cambridge.org.